The Lambí's Call:

A Haitian Journey

Tom Fame

About the Title: The Lambi (conch shell) is the Haitian symbol of freedom and hope. It was blown during the Haitian slave revolt by the nèg mawon, the freed man, and its call still brings Haitians together today.

The Nèg Mawon
Port-au-Prince, Haiti. Near the National Palace

The Lambi's Call:

A Haitian Journey

Tom Fame

Published in the United States of America
by: Trust Publisher
P.O. Box 872
Salem VA 24153

Cover design and photographs by Tom Fame

Library and publication data:

Fame, Tom
The Lambi's Call: A Haitian Journey /
by Tom Fame
p. cm.
Includes discussion questions.

ISBN: 978-0-615-22003-1
1. Humanitarian. 2. Schools – Haiti.
3. Parish twinning. I. Title

Library of Congress Control Number: 2008907844

2nd Printing
Printed in the United States of America
Bookmasters: Ashland, OH

For the people of Haiti,
to whom this book is dedicated,
may their spirit for life and their endless hope
continue to instruct and inspire us all.

About the Author:

Tom Fame is a physician with a practice of allergy and immunology in Salem, Virginia. Since 1996 he has worked in the central plateau region of Haiti as the founder and chair of the O.L.P.H. Haiti Project. He has spoken extensively on Haiti to church and civic groups. As a Secular Franciscan, he has committed himself to working in Haiti. In 2008 Dr. Fame started planning a clean water project for the people of the Cabestor Valley, and is now studying to receive his Masters of Public Health from the Johns Hopkins Bloomberg School of Public Health in Baltimore, Maryland. He hopes to incorporate a satellite health clinic with Zanmi Lasante Haiti in the future.

This book chronicles the building of the relationship between the author and the people of Haiti, as it shows the genesis of the schools and other projects he has been involved in.

Dr. Fame presently lives in Salem, Virginia with his wife Leah. He has three daughters, Ryann, Rachel, and Michelle, who have all visited Haiti as well. Proceeds from the sale of this book go to sustain the long term funding of this Haiti Project. Dr. Fame is available for lectures, and book signings through Trust Publisher or O.L.P.H. Haiti Project (see back of book).

Acknowledgements

Thanks go to my wife, Leah, and to my daughters, Ryann, Rachel, and Michelle for allowing me to share my love for them with my love for the people of Haiti. Leah had also patiently read and reread the manuscript, editing it many times during the writing process.

I would like to thank Bishop Emeritus Walter F. Sullivan for his foresight and courage in leading the members of the Diocese of Richmond beyond our comfort levels, and beyond our borders to work with the people of Hinche, in Haiti's Central Plateau. Also, to Adele and Bob DellaValle-Rauth for their work to help make Bishop Sullivan's dream a reality. They have been tireless advocates for Haiti, and for the idea of working in solidarity with the people of Haiti. Please read their foreword to this book.

Thanks to Jean and Tommy Denton who have been constant partners on many of our trips to Haiti. Both of them are real writers, who have been supportive and reassuring to me during the writing of this book. I thank Jean for her help with the layout and any artwork found within this book, and her editorial assistance.

A special thanks to all of my Franciscan brothers and sisters around the world, but especially the members of The Companions of Francis and Clare Secular Franciscan fraternity in Roanoke, Virginia. Especially Marsha Dubose who has always been so positive and encouraging from the beginning.

To all the parishioners of Our Lady of Perpetual Help Catholic Church in Salem Virginia who have supported this project, and to all the leaders who have guided the twinned parishes program in Virginia, and around the U.S.

To the many priests who have helped encourage me here in the United States and in Haiti. Bishop Emeritus Walter F. Sullivan,

Monsignor Tom Miller, Father Gregory Kandt, and Father Remi Sojka who have all put up with my non-stop questions and requests regarding Haiti. Father Polinice Daisma, and Father Hermann Heriveaux who you will read about in this book, and the many priests throughout Haiti, and the Diocese of Hinche whose daily works help to improve the lives of these poor but not forgotten people of Haiti.

Thanks also to Hector, Yves, Watson, and all the folks at Marie's Caribbean Creole for the support I've received from the Roanoke Haitian community. And for all the people of Haiti, to whom this book is dedicated, and for all that they have taught me. May their spirit and their endless hope continue to instruct and inspire us all.

Adele, Pè Pol, Pè Hermann, and Tom.

Contents

Foreword

Adele DellaValle-Rauth, M.S., M.A.

I have been privileged to witness Tom Fame's Haitian journey practically from "day one." I vividly recall this man on fire with youthful energy bursting into a meeting room at his parish, as my husband and I were introducing members of his Justice and Peace group to the idea of twinning. We hoped for a warm and receptive audience and got much more than that because of Tom. He had just developed photos of his latest medical mission to Haiti. He eagerly passed the photos around, regaling us at the same time with the wonders of Haiti and the people who had found a place in his heart. Somehow in the midst of the destitution and squalor, which Haitians endure, Tom saw a pearl of great price – God in his neighbor.

On subsequent missions Tom left his medical kit behind. He wanted nothing to come between him and the people, often saying he wanted to "be", not "do", and continued his healing ministry in a direct, personal manner. In the years since 1998 he has nevertheless translated his love of God and neighbor from word to action. This book chronicles the journey that has consumed his life. Along the way he has become a student of Haitian culture and history and learned their language of Haitian Kreyòl. If ever there was a "natif natal" (native Haitian) at heart, it is Tom.

Tom's personal transformation was just the beginning. He has doggedly inspired and moved the people of his parish of Our Lady of Perpetual Help to a deeply rewarding twinning relationship. It has been a journey of accompaniment, with Tom leading person after person, parishioners, friends, as well as every member of his family – virtually tantalizing anyone within his radar screen - to experience an immersion in Haiti. The people of Lascahobas have been the beneficiaries. They are known and loved by name. It is one thing to give money to the poor, to pray for the sick and the suffering. It is another to put oneself in their place, to join hands, to walk with them as friend and brother/sister. A relationship of profound mutual trust develops. That is the essence of twinning and the meaning of solidarity. One natural response to twinning with Haiti is the recognition of the disparity of wealth. In this recognition twinning assumes a sharing of material goods but one will see in these pages how the spiritual wealth of the people of Haiti enrich all who encounter them. Having nothing, they hold nothing back. The words friendship and hospitality acquire a whole new dimension, beyond imagination.

Anyone who has been to Haiti knows the difficulty of travel. I remember a Haitian once telling me that there was "no road" to his home in northern Haiti. I thought he exaggerated until I went myself and found this to be true! Tom describes how, together with his Haitian pastor and the support of many others, a brand new school was built in an extremely remote chapel area – and then the road was constructed. Sometimes, in a country like Haiti you travel uncharted territory – and may put the cart before the horse!

Reading this book will evoke tears, laughter, and sometimes awe. Tom's Haiti is a country of miracles. Recently a Haitian pastor said, "We Haitians have a secret weapon – joy in the midst of unbelievable suffering." The Haitian smile is contagious. At bottom, we are all alike. And in this common humanity lies the motivation for reaching out and sharing. I invite you, dear reader, to sit back, relax, and fasten your seat belt for the ride of your life from the pen and the heart of chronicler: Tom Fame.

Adele DellaValle-Rauth served as the Haiti Twinning Resource for the Diocese of Richmond for ten years, and is Founder, together with her husband Bob, of the 20-year twinning relationship at Resurrection Church, Moneta with a girls' orphanage, the Foyer des Filles de Dieu, in Port-au-Prince

August, 2008

CUBA
Cap-Haitien
HAITI
Hinche
Lake Peligre
Gonaives
Artibonite R.
Belladaire
Lascahobas
Mirebalais
Port-au-Prince
Dominican
Republic

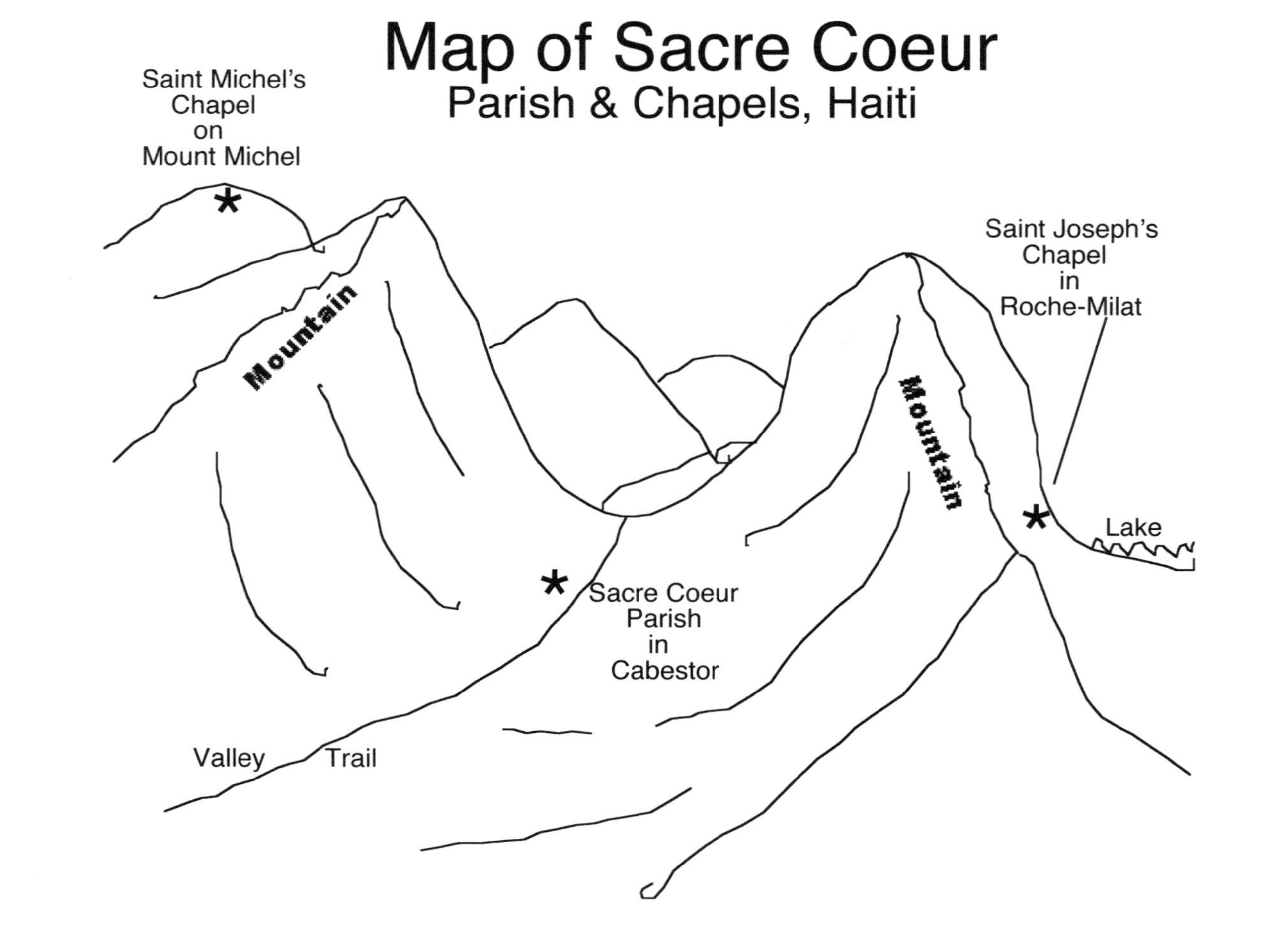
Map of Sacre Coeur
Parish & Chapels, Haiti
Saint Michel's Chapel on Mount Michel
Mountain
Saint Joseph's Chapel in Roche-Milat
Mountain
Lake
Sacre Coeur Parish in Cabestor
Valley Trail

1
Living the Dream

Depi Lambi konen, tout moun konnen, sak pral genyen.
Se nouvel Ayisyen, nouvel ki soti byen lwen.

When the Lambi sounds, everybody knows what is going to happen.
It is Haitian news, good news that comes from far away.

Looking out at the morning sky, I could see the sun breaking open the dark clouds, which had rained throughout the night. As I stood in the doorway of the rectory looking out at the churchyard, it was a new day of the New Year: January 1, 2001. We were preparing to leave the rectory of St Gabriel's Parish in Lascahobas, Haiti for the dedication of the new Sacre Coeur School. I was hoping for a nicer day, but wouldn't it be just like Haiti to 'rain on your parade.' This is a day that has been building up to a crescendo since 1996 when we began this project, this relationship with the community of St. Gabriel's here in the Central Plateau of Haiti, the poorest country in the Western Hemisphere.

It seems like that description 'the poorest country in the Western Hemisphere' always follows the name 'Haiti' as if it were its family name. In the same way that 'Christ' the anointed one, always follows Jesus' name: Jesus Christ. This actually might not be such a bad analogy, since just as Jesus needed to be crucified to become the anointed one, so it seems to be with Haiti. Materially one of the poorest, one of the most left behind, one of the most used and abused countries in our world, and yet in spite of it, and maybe because of it: filled with some of the richest people I have ever meet.

But on this day we would have no talk of despair, no talk of pain, today would be a day of rejoicing, of celebrating and of new hope. Not only because it is Haitian Independence day, a new year, and the feast of Peace in the Church, but because this community would open a new school in Cabestor. The completion of this school is an event that I initially thought would never happen. There were so many obstacles; finding the money, learning to trust Pè Hermann, and getting the materials and work done out in Cabestor, this very remote part of Haiti outside of Lascahobas.

The town of Lascahobas is a small village with about 6,000 residents; it has a long main street that winds through town with several side streets branching off it. All of these streets seem to lead into a central square with the large St. Gabriel's Church on one side of the square, and the police station (built on the grounds of an ancient dilapidated prison) across from it. The surface of these streets had just recently been covered with paving stones to help cut down on the ever-present 'labou,' mud, which finds its way into everything during the rainy season. These same streets seem to be constantly filled with life as if it were a moving theater. People travel up and down all day long, mostly on foot, but some on bikes, a few riding mules, motorcycles, and the rare car. The vehicles are all dirty and banged up reflecting the hard life of the people and the country roads. Everyone seems to be on a mission; heading to school or to market or some activity, but still they will find the time to say "Bonjou," good-morning, and bring up a smile for you.

Lascahobas is a beautiful little village that is surrounded by mountains that are green, but not heavily forested. A small patch of smoke can be seen rising from the misty hillside on this new morning, probably someone preparing their land for planting, or perhaps they are making some 'chabon' or charcoal, which is the main fuel source of rural Haiti.

You could smell the smoke through the heavy, damp morning air. Most of that smell was coming from the small kitchen across the yard from the rectory, where several women have been busy throughout the night preparing the food we will be taking to the dedication. Even after all their work, they still found time to make us some good Haitian coffee, and I could see Santa walking over to us in the rectory, carrying a tray with a large pot and some cups. Santa is a Haitian girl about ten years old, who has a very wide welcoming smile, with somewhat bashful down gazing eyes. Her hair is in short, corn rowed braids, which flopped in different directions over her head. The church took her in to help Justine and Chantal in the kitchen in exchange for schooling and support.

"Bonjou Santa." I said.

"Bonjou." She replied quietly while placing the heavy tray carefully and skillfully onto the large dinner table in the rectory's common room. Then with an awkward giggle she quickly scampered back to the safety of the kitchen and the other Haitian women. There she would tell her story of surviving her encounter with the 'blan,' the white person, or as I would find out later, any non-Haitian visitor.

It seems that the smell of the coffee brought the rest of the blans in our group down as well. "Good morning everyone." I greeted them all as they made their way to the coffee and stack of cups on the table. From this large common eating and meeting room in the rectory I could see the young Haitian men loading up the two Land Rovers in the yard right outside the door.

"Good morning Ryann." I said to my 17-year-old daughter who was making her first of several trips to Haiti. "Did you sleep well?"

"Wi papa, domi byen." Ryann replied in her best Kreyòl. "It took a while to get used to the street noises, and the barking dogs, roosters, and fighting cats throughout the night. I finally got some sleep until woken at five by the church bells right across from our room."

"Byenveni Ayiti!" I chuckled back. Then seeing it was getting to be time, I asked, "Hey, is everyone ready?"

"Yeah." "Sure." "Let's go!" They all replied with a mix of excitement and insomnia.

"I saw Father Hermann a while ago." I informed the group, "He's been up and down directing the loading. We should be ready to leave in about an hour, Haitian time. So get yourselves a quick breakfast before then."

We were a group of 11 including myself, and four teens, all here to witness the school dedication, and to experience life in Haiti. Most of us were from Salem, Virginia and the sister parish of Our Lady of Perpetual Help. The teens have all seemed to adjust readily to Haitian kids and did not seem to be affected that much by the poverty around us. Ryann's French skills were actually quite good for conversation, so she was dubbed 'bouch Tom,' or Tom's mouthpiece by Pè Hermann.

For many in the group, this was their first time to Haiti or to any third world country, and a few were having a difficult time coping with the sights and smells of the poverty. Especially difficult for many was the experience in Port-au-Prince of holding and feeding the sick and dying infants at Mother Teresa's Hospital. Looking into the sunken hollow eyes of a two year old the size of a six month old, who doesn't have the strength to eat, no less breathe through their wheezing, thin ribbed tuberculin chest wall is an experience that not many can walk away from unchanged. Those women were very somber and quiet for the rest of the trip after that experience, and had trouble retelling the story later. It was only at the dedication ceremony that I finally saw their faces brighten with some hope. Once they saw the new school, they understood.

I started to hear the volume of voices and the commotion pick up out in the churchyard. "I think Pè Hermann is getting ready to go." I told the rest of the group. I have learned to listen and be ready when Pè Hermann says it is time. He is the boss in Lascahobas, and over the years I have found that to be a good guest is to allow him that respect and position.

The small churchyard outside the rectory is flanked by, the back of the church, the quarters for the parish workers and kitchen, and the exit gate. This morning the yard was just about filled with the two vehicles and about twenty people helping to get things ready. We all started squeezing into the Land Rovers as the young Haitian men finished packing the last minute supplies in and on top of the vehicles. We made quite a parade leaving the town, but a lot of the local folks had already started down the road to Cabestor, most walking, with a few of the lucky ones riding mules.

On the way out we passed the town's graveyard, and John joked saying, "I hope this isn't a bad omen." We knew when we had hit the town limits because we dropped off the paving stones and onto the rocky dirt road that led down to the Lascahobas River. Without a bridge, we passed through and across the river, which was high after the night's rain, but still passable. The rest of the nine Kilometer trip was quite bouncy and rattling, 'shake and bake,' I think someone called it. But, if you took the time to look around at the mountains along the valley, and at the gardens and palm trees, you would see just how beautiful this part of Haiti is. Just like all the people we passed along the way.

Ryann was riding in the back of the car and was starting to look a bit concerned about the conditions of the wet, widened trail we were using as a road that day. Especially when we would cross down and up the many gullies and streams along the way. A young Haitian man named Mara saw Ryann's worried face and asked her, "Gyel." (Gyel is Ryann's Haitian name) "Gyel, are you afraid?"

"A little bit." She bravely replied while holding onto the car for dear life.

"Don't be afraid Gyel." Mara said reassuringly, "We have a good car, and a good driver, and a good God, together they will get us there."

And sure enough, we did arrive at the church field of Sacre Coeur Chapel and School. It was a lively welcoming scene of about one thousand slightly damp but excited Haitians cheering our arrival and greeting us with, "Bon Ane!" Happy New Year! Ryann was quite surprised when after the car stopped, about five young Haitian men came dropping off the top of the car down past her window.

"I didn't know they were up there! Oh my gosh, I can't believe they rode all the way from town up on top of this car!" She exclaimed, with both her mouth and eyes equally wide open.

Out on the church grounds, there were groups of Haitians obviously from the country, but dressed in the finest clothes they could put together. I have always wondered how they are able to make it over these trails and dusty or muddy roads and still keep their clothes looking clean. I saw lots of children running around and playing under the large mango trees by the church.

Sacre Coeur Chapel is a nicely built stone church whose community is a separate part of the greater St Gabriel's Parish proper. It does not have a full time priest of its own; Pè Hermann is responsible for looking after this and eight other chapels. There is a large yard for gathering, and for playing soccer, and then on the other side of the field across from the church was the new Sacre Coeur School. Freshly painted white and grey, and decorated for the festival, its presence stood as a symbol of hope shining through the damp weather that day. When I looked at the school surrounded by all of this life, I had the same overwhelming sense of pride and happiness that I experienced after the birth of my first child. And later I would find that this community had become part of my family.

The school was not much of a structure by western standards, cinderblock and tin roof construction, but out here in the forgotten back lands of this Haitian countryside, it was as if the University of Virginia had been dropped down into Cabestor. That is how this community saw it. There is not a great system of public education even in the major Haitian cities, so you can pretty much forget about finding schools out here in the country. Today you could see the hope in people's eyes, and the excitement about the coming celebration.

There were people who came from all over the Central Plateau. They visited from Lascahobas, Mirebalais, and the main city: Hinche. People had hiked from over the mountains that surrounded the lush Cabestor valley, and from the surrounding rural home sites. There were even Spanish speakers from across the border of the Dominican Republic. I asked them, "Why are you here? It's just the opening of a little school."

They replied, "This is a BIG thing for a school to open, plus we heard there was a party."

Pè Hermann was getting things in place near the church, and he had changed into his vestments. I saw two rows of neatly dressed barefoot girls wearing white robes with gold ribbons around their waists and heads. They looked precious, and were ready to offer up what they could, their dance, for the occasion.

With Hermann's signal we were ushered into the church to be seated in our places of honor up by the altar. With so many people out in the yard, I was surprised to see that the inside of the church was already packed with people waiting to begin. I could not help noticing a man wearing a suit and sitting in the front row with his beautifully exotic looking Haitian wife. His name was Phillip and he appeared to be 15 years her elder. He was a local dignitary, and I remembered seeing Phillip's compound along the trail to Cabestor on other trips. They asked me afterwards if I would take some family photos and bring them copies on future trips. I would later find that it was hard to pass by Phillip's house on our way to Cabestor, without stopping by for a visit with him and his family.

The Mass proceeded with singing from all of the loud joyful voices; the choir as well as the congregation. All of this music was lead by the rhythmic accents of drums, makeshift guitars, and trumpets. That along with the young barefoot dancers, gesturing their arms with praise to heaven, was enough to bring a tear to my eyes. They have nothing, really, but they can give what they have, their bodies in dance or song. And give it they did. During the offertory, the young dancers came gyrating down the aisle, advancing in spurts and stops, with all types of fruits and tubers and bananas as well as live chickens and Guinea Hens in baskets balanced atop their heads. It was a spectacular sight and celebration.

I was told beforehand to make a presentation in Kreyòl, but my language skills had not yet advanced to the point where I could say what I really wanted to say in their common language: Haitian Kreyòl. The night before I wrote down my words in English, and Pè Wilcoxson, the associate priest working with Hermann, helped me with the translation. It went like this:

"Bonjou tout moun. (Good morning everyone.) I hope that everyone is fine today. Happy New Year to Cabestor, Haiti, we are all so happy to be here on this special day. We are visiting with you all today for the blessing of this new school. Father Hermann wanted me to speak to you all about this new school, but before I do that, I would like to tell you a little story about Mary and the baby Jesus. God announced to Mary, "I am going to give you a son." And soon afterwards Mary gave birth to the baby Jesus, but the baby was not for her, the baby was sent from God for everyone. When I had visited Cabestor the first time with Father Pol, God spoke to us as well, and He told us that through the love of our two communities, we were going to have a baby as well. Our baby is this school. I have watched the baby grow now into an infant with the help of Father Hermann, but this baby is not mine. This baby, this school is from God, and He made it for all of the people in Cabestor. God made this school for you all because you have kept a strong faith, because you have loved each other, and because you have been praying faithfully. God has heard your prayers, and this school is his response to you all. Today we are going to baptize this baby, with a blessing by Fr. Hermann of the school. May God continue to watch over this school, and all of the people in Cabestor that it will serve. Thank you, and God bless you."

They clapped in appreciation and apparent understanding, and then the service began to wind down. I didn't think that I could be any more amazed until we experienced the ending of the ceremony. There is no way to describe it other than total joyous mayhem. I could not help but be swept up in the energy of the moment and started to shake and jump with the congregation. How happy. How cathartic and emotionally expressive of the celebration that continued as we poured out into the yard and to a sunnier day than when we arrived. I went with Hermann to the school with choir in tow, and after a short ceremony he blessed the school. He baptized it by sprinkling water shaken from a bundle of leaves he had dipped into a basin. The hope in the eyes of the people that day was indescribable. I saw children laughing and blowing bubbles, young and old people dancing, some with my wife Leah; black and white, Haitian and American together, sharing this common experience of the understood joy that comes from the gift of hope.

There were even some members from the local press there, if you can call them that; they had a microphone and a home camcorder asking questions about the project and our group. People were passing out a clear intoxicating liquid that I recognized as moonshine since we come from southwest

Virginia. I found out later that they call it 'Kleren' and this particular batch was less than clear given all the small particles floating in it. So I decided to take what my wife calls a 'no thank you portion' to be hospitable, but skip the hospital.

At midday a huge soccer game broke out between many of the young people. Towards the end of the day I remember seeing a couple dancing; they were an older country couple by the weathered look of their skin and clothing. A simple couple, and I am sure that if I could have gotten their entire history, I would have heard a tale as hard and as desperate as the road we had just traveled to Cabestor. Yet here, on this day, at this celebration, they appeared relaxed and at peace. Their eyes a little red from too much drink, but gazing at each other the way only a long-married couple can. Their faces had a look of contentment and hope that spoke as if to say, "We know that our lives have been hard and are almost over, but we can leave this world knowing that things will be better for our grandchildren because they will have a chance to get an education."

The celebration went on well into the night. Jean Denton, one of our long time Haiti voyagers whose teen son Luke and daughter Libby were also with us, came up to me and stated what was obvious but so true. "You must feel really proud today. You've worked so hard to get this dream of theirs realized, and nobody thought it was possible except for you and the people here in Haiti." I told Jean that Haitians are used to living with impossible dreams. One of the things they have taught me is to have faith and trust that these impossible dreams can be realized. And here we were today touching that first dream: there would be more.

2
Zombie

Makak pa janm kwè petit-li lèd.

A monkey never thinks her baby is ugly.

I feel sometimes like I live a duel life. One rooted here in Salem, Virginia, and another life with my friends and the community in Haiti. It has been several years now since we all experienced the excitement of that day with the school's dedication. I remember thinking about it as a baptism back then. Now, as time has passed and the journey continues, my relationship with this community in Haiti has matured, more like a marriage. The honeymoon has long been over. Now the hard work of building and sustaining our friendship has begun, through time spent working together and understanding each other. People here at home can sense a change in my priorities and how I spend my time, and there is a curiosity about what is going on down there in Haiti. A reporter from The Roanoke Times called me last week and wanted to come over to write a story about the project. I am expecting her visit, but I am not sure what I will say. It is at times like these when I ask myself, "Tom, what are you doing in Haiti?"

The young reporter arrived. "Hi Mr. Fame, or is it Doctor?" she asked as we tried to find a place where we could talk.

"Tom is fine. Why don't we sit here at my desk, it'll be easier for you to take notes."

This obviously was not a big news story from the looks of the twenty-something reporter that was sent, a red haired, pony tailed young woman who appeared to be fresh out of college. Still she asked some good questions, and seemed very professional and organized.

"Well Mr. Fame, I think I understand what you all have been up to with this Haiti project. But I'm curious, can you tell me how you went from working as a physician in Virginia to this project in Haiti?"

"Well. That's a good question. Let me think." I told her as I tried to recall how this all began. When did it start? I had to go back a bit in my mind.

It was the early 90's and I had been volunteering regularly at the Bradley Free Clinic in Roanoke. Estelle Nichols is its longtime director and foundress of this 'Free Clinic for the working poor.' The Free Clinic movement had its beginning in the Haight-Ashbury neighborhood of San Francisco in the late 60's, and this particular clinic in Roanoke is known as one of the most successful from those humble days. Estelle is its heart and its life. Physicians, nurses, pharmacists, and other volunteers provide free medical care to the working uninsured.

Jean Broyles, a longtime local nurse who has done just about everything in nursing, was working the clinic one night while I was there. I always enjoyed myself at the free clinic. Hey, you were working overtime for free; you might as well have fun. Some people appreciate a little silliness more than others; Jean was one of those people. As we were finishing our notes up at the counter, I overheard Jean talking about a medical trip to Jamaica.

I have always thought that I would like to volunteer overseas. I asked Jean. "What's this about a trip to Jamaica? It sounds like fun, but I'm not sure you'd need an allergist to go. What about pediatrics?"

"That'd be great Tom, there should be lots of kids to see." Jean said with her usual energetic smile.

Jean was a great organizer and motivator. She had been on several Mission Trips with the United Methodist Church, and this was just another one for her. She assembled a great team of doctors, nurses, dentists, and an optometrist to go. After months of planning, boxing up meds and supplies, and bonding, we headed off to Jamaica. It was my first trip to the Caribbean, and I remember flying over Cuba. "Are we allowed to do this?" I asked, thinking that we really should not be flying over a communist country. I doubt Castro really cared.

We spent a week in Jamaica, sleeping and eating in a home in Kingston. I remember the heat and humidity, and how exotic it all seemed. So different, all of the houses had high cinderblock walls around them, with sharp shattered pieces of glass on the tops to keep people from climbing over them. If that was not enough security, you could hear the loud barking of the mean sounding dogs growling at the gates. Once while jogging past a similar home with an unlocked gate, I saw two flesh-ripping pit bulls come running out after me. There was nothing I could do but freeze in the middle of the street, thinking that by running I would only make their sport more exciting. So I stood there stiffened as they bounded towards me, only to have them stop, bark a bit, and then just walk past on either side of me as if all was forgotten. "AAAHHH!" I howled to myself. Note to self: save the exercise for when you get home.

The clinic was high up in the Blue Mountains of Jamaica's coffee country. I was told that these mountains rose to over 7,000 feet, and that's with us starting from sea level in Kingston. The first day we traveled in a thick fog. I could not see what was around us, but I knew that we were climbing by how steep and winding the road was.

At the clinic, we were given a chair, a small table, and about 100 patients to see. It was chaotic, hot, frustrating work, made more difficult without all the fancy tools available to doctors in the U.S. Still, just being able to lay hands on, and to look into the eyes of so many of these forgotten children and their parents was very moving. At lunch we took a break and walked outside the clinic, the fog had lifted and I could not believe what we saw. The building was right on the side of a very steep mountain. The view was as spectacular as was the steepness of the drop-off. Besides the vertigo, the beauty of the sharp, mist-collared peaks across the way was breathtaking. It made us forget about all the work we had done that day.

We went back to that and other rural clinics each day, and we worked just as hard and as franticly. As good Americans we felt it was our duty to see everyone, and not stop working until everything was done. We were tired; I remember how hard the eyeglass team worked to get one of the last clients of the day a pair of glasses: she had a particularly difficult prescription. Finally after searching through boxes of Lions Club donations, they found just the right ones. Or so they thought.

"How can you see with these glasses?" Dr. Dave asked, both pleased and exhausted after the hunt.

"Well sir." The elderly lady replied in her best Jamaican accent. "I can sees well e-noff; but do yas tink yas has any in pink?"

The team, looking sweaty and worn from the long week, had facial expressions as if to say they were not thinking good thoughts. I believe she settled for what she got, and walked on home, still unhappy and going over it all a bit under her breath.

It was a great week of shared work, some frustration, and of touching people who really appreciated just the fact that we were there. We arrived home feeling like we had saved the world. That is how we saw it anyways. After telling stories of our trip and of all the care we gave out, one of my physician colleagues, an orthopedist who seemed to always bring up the cynical point of view asked sarcastically, "Well, that sounds nice. But what did you REALLY do down there? How are their lives different now that you're home?"

I was put off a bit by this, and thought, "Well this guy's really a lot of fun." But it was a question that stayed with me for a while, and I would hear him asking me this question again in my mind.

The next year when a similar trip to Haiti was planned, I was ready. People came to talk to us about how the poverty in Haiti was ten times worse than what we saw in Jamaica. They warned us that if we were not prepared for what we would see, we might find it hard to work there. We went through the same preparation as we did for Jamaica, and I remember that we spent $25,000 on medications and I thought that this seemed like a lot of money. I wondered if we could have used that much money to do something that would have a more permanent effect in Haiti.

We flew by Lynx Air into Cap-Haitien, the northernmost city in Haiti. Lynx Air is owned and flown by two pilots who fly a small 14-seat turbo-prop out of Fort Lauderdale, Florida. Like most pilots, they liked to joke and hot dog. Our descent into Cap-Haitien was rather steep and rapid. They made an announcement just before landing that the weather was going to be hot and humid, and for local time, turn your clocks back 200 years.

The Cap-Haitien airport, take note that this is Haiti's second largest city, was just a landing strip with one small building all surrounded by a chain link fence. We picked our bags up from the tarmac where they had been thrown off the back of the plane. We carried them to a large table under a tin roof held up by four large tree poles; there they were ruffled through by these Haitian men in ripped shirts and raggedy clothes. Even with their airport ID badges, we really were not sure if they were official. Outside, people were hanging onto the fence, with their faces ogling at us through the chain links of the gate. I think they wanted to find a job helping us with bags or to sell drinks. Others were waiting for the mail that Lynx Air carries from Florida; many of these letters contain money that relatives send to help their families living in Haiti.

The drive to the hotel fulfilled all of the prior predictions of Haiti's poverty. We saw streets packed with people walking barefoot or with ratty, worn-out shoes. Thin muscular men were carrying heavy loads on their shoulders or in wheelbarrows. They carried on their backs stacks of heavy wooden boards, sacks of charcoal, engine parts, and much more. I didn't know that the human body could sustain this kind of work. Women carried similar heavy loads, but balanced carefully on their heads. The work was equally as hard, but it gave them a sort of grace and dignified look as they walked. I was later told that it was easier to list the things that women did not carry on their heads in Haiti. The streets were dirty, crowded, and hot, but I did not see much fighting or arguing. They seemed to be tired, but just accepting and accustomed to this hard way of life.

As we passed through the city center, the crowds of pedestrians became more dense and dangerous with cars and people packed together. On the sides of the roads there were sparks flying from men welding steel rods to make furniture and other products right on the curbside. Occasionally a fire was seen from burning trash or a charcoal stove. The smoke made for an eerie scene with people appearing in and out of, or partially covered by the smoke clouds as they were walking by. You can see the past beauty of Cap-Haitien's New Orleans style buildings. High narrow shuttered doors and windows, with wrought iron balconies above. The piles of uncollected garbage and the buildings' disrepair spoke of a grandeur long past.

We arrived at Beck's Hotel; a large hillside complex owned by an elderly but very gracious German-Haitian man named Kurt Beck. He and his younger Haitian companion Michaela served as our hosts. With Herr Beck's German accent, and the lush tropical setting of the hotel, complete with wicker ceiling fans, it really made it seem like we were in a 1940's movie. It was much more relaxing and peaceful at the hotel than what we had seen on our way from the airport. The disparity between the hardness of the street life, and the luxury and prosperity of the hotel painted a contrasting picture of life in what I would learn are the two Haiti's.

Herr Beck has lived in Cap-Haitien his entire life. He told us of how in his youth he directed the building of the Hotel using Haitian artisans, and he seems to have found a way to make a nice living in Haiti with several enterprises. Twenty-five years ago he planted 2,000 mahogany trees, which he was now harvesting for various wood products. To think that far ahead really takes planning and patience, especially given that Herr Beck seemed to be in his late 70's.

We found out that he and I both belonged to Rotary International, so Herr Beck took me to one of their club meetings to meet other local businessmen. The speaker that day was a Haitian national living in Montreal who was just hired as the director of the Cap-Haitien beautification department. His first job, he told us, "Would be to pick up all the uncollected garbage around the city."

That sounded reasonable. I could not help but think, somewhat jokingly, "I guess that the planting of rosebushes in the parks and at the city entrances would have to wait."

Herr Beck arranged our transportation out to the rural clinic in Latannerie. The young Haitian men who were helping us knew some English, and since none of us knew Haitian Kreyòl, they would act as our interpreters. As we exited through the hotel gate, there was a large metal water tank surrounded by older, uniformed, Haitian students standing and facing the side of the tank wall. "I need to find out what that is about later," I told myself. But for now we were headed out past the same street scene with all its busy-ness. The chaos seemed to lessen as we made our way out into the country with its mountains and fields of banana trees, mango trees, and coconuts.

The Latannerie clinic was located along the road, overlooking the Grande Rivière du Nord. My first thought was, what a beautiful place. Then I saw all the people in a line stretching out for hundreds of yards waiting for us. They were mostly women and children who had been waiting since early that morning. They had heard that 'the white doctors,' the blans, were coming today.

There is a Haitian joke I was told about 'the white doctor,' I think it tells a lot about Haitian perceptions. It goes like this:

There was a terrible auto accident in Port-au-Prince, many cars and people were hit and lay bleeding out on the street. Walking by was a 'white doctor' who started triaging the injured. "He's ok. He's ok. He's injured. He's dead." The blan said.

Then the Haitian man who was pronounced dead lifted his head and spoke up, "Hey, wait. I'm not dead! I'm ok, really."

When another Haitian man heard this he said, "Be quiet you and lie down there, if the blan says you're dead, then you're dead!"

So the blans were here, now what? Over the five-day clinic we saw hundreds of patients each. Most of the children suffered from intestinal worms and malnutrition. Many of them would complain that they 'eat dirt,' which has a medical term: pica. You learn about this in medical school, pica is a sign of advanced anemia, but I don't think that I have ever seen it in the states. After a while I stopped checking their hematocrits because so many of these kids were very anemic, and I just started treating them all with iron & vitamins. It seems that the anemia is due to a combination of poor nutrition; combined with their worms that cause intestinal losses, through bleeding, of the little iron they get.

One little infant was brought in barely alive, dehydrated, sunken eyes, semi-conscious with shallow breathing. The mother looked terrified at her newborn, "Please help him. I can't make any milk for him." She told us. We could not even start an I.V. for fluid, so the nurses took turns over two days feeding him dropper by dropper. The baby finally perked up, but here was a little child who had almost died not from the lack of any advanced medical procedure or new medication, but due to a lack of the most basics of care: infant formula and clean water.

After awhile I came to realize that there were no other medical resources available out here, and there would not be any follow-up after we left. For that reason we could only treat people with problems that could be helped with the few medicines we brought with us. Even these treatable problems could only be continued for about a month until the medications we provided ran out. I saw a boy with a fairly significant heart murmur; I asked if there was any way to treat this in Haiti?

"You've got to be kidding!" was the reply from our Haitian friends.

I decided not to tell the mother anything, "He's fine." I said. Why cause them any worry, he is not showing any signs of illness, and there isn't anything we can do for it. I could see what little control I really had over things. I realized that most of the 'power' that comes from being a physician in the U.S. comes from 'the system' of medicine that has been built up, with all of its technology and skilled technicians backing you up. None of that was here in Haiti; a different approach was needed to address the massive systemic failures that were around us.

I enjoyed looking into the faces and eyes of all of these children and their mothers, they were so patient waiting out in the sun all day and I never once saw anyone complain or get angry with their children. My Haitian interpreter Ronald did not fare as well, becoming very tired and slumping more and more as the day was ending. I would ask him to translate a question such as, "Are you having any trouble urinating?"

Then I would hear this long and lively exchange between Ronald and the mother. Finally, after a couple of minutes Ronald would reply, "Pi-pi ok."

"What!" I'd exclaimed. "There's no way all of that talk was just for 'pi-pi ok.'"

Towards the end of the day the men would start to come in since they were done with their work. The most common complaint was, 'Pain all over.' Now as a physician trying to come up with a differential diagnosis for a complaint of 'pain all over' is just a little hard to pin down. I was getting frustrated, and it took me several days of talking to understand something about how Haitians think about their bodies. First they do not have a history of going to the doctor, and they just do not think much about the specifics of what their body is telling them, like we do. All of that talk with Ronald about 'pi-pi ok' was just from the mom's frustration about the question in the first place.

"Why are you asking that ridiculous question?" They would reply. "Are you Haitian or what? My child is just sick. Just tell the blan to give us some medicine."

And the men would say, 'pain all over,' because if you took the time to look around, and if you paid any attention to how hard these men worked all day long, carrying things through the streets and up and down those mountains, you would have pain all over too!

One of the more unique encounters I had was with a cute little teenage girl about sixteen years old who was complaining of 'Zombie.' It appears that she was having some sort of passing out spells, but the story was a little strange. Still I wanted to make sure it was not a seizure or a cardiac event. I asked her to describe for me what other people who had witnessed her attacks saw.

"Well," she said, "My teeth grow long and pointed with blood pouring out of my eyes, nose and mouth, then I start spitting out fire."

"Hmmmm." I told myself, "I guess I can rule out seizures at this point." It turns out that 'zombie' is a voodoo curse that someone had placed on her. "Well what do I have in my medical bag for this?" I thought. Luckily I brought some bright colorful rope friendship bracelets as gifts for the kids. I pulled out one of these bracelets in a very solemn and ceremonious fashion, and I told her, "This bracelet has the power to undo zombie. If you wear it, and take the pills I will give you (vitamins), your zombie will be gone from you." It was all done in a very dramatic way, with sweeping hand gestures for effect. She cried some, and smiled as if a great weight had been lifted from her. We hugged and she bounced off happy in her new found freedom. Although the other doctors laughed at this story, in a few days they began asking me for some of those 'zombie bracelets' as well.

In the afternoon of the final day of our clinic, a small riot started up outside where people were being checked in. People were starting to get upset when they were told that there would be no more check-ins, and that these latecomers could not be seen. People had been promised that we would see everyone who came that day. To prevent W.W. III, we agreed to work longer until everyone was seen. It is hard sometimes to provide a short-term service in Haiti, because inevitably the question comes up: when do you stop? Is it worse to do a little and then take it away, or to do nothing at all? I started to ask questions about what our commitment to the Haitian people really was. Were we really there as deeply caring and committed people, or was this just a nice experience for a week?

On our day off, I became curious about life beyond the gates of the Beck's Hotel. I walked out to see what those students were doing in front of the water tank each morning. The way they were facing the wall of the tank, I really thought that the boys were relieving themselves. It turned out that they were doing homework. Since they did not have enough pens or paper, they were using white chalky rocks to write on the tank as if it was a chalkboard. I was impressed by the complexity of the chemistry and algebra problems that they were working on. I have to admit that it uncovered in me a misperception that I held. It revealed that I had a prejudiced mindset about Haitians before seeing this. I had never really seen Haitians as educated people, it was a subconscious thought I realized, but still it was there: not anymore. Could you see an American teen waking up early to walk to a water tank to do their chemistry and math homework?

A few minutes later I heard a band playing down the street, it was at one of the Catholic schools, and these kids were celebrating the feast day of their school with a parade of brass instruments and drums. It was great seeing the joy of these young people in the midst of their hard lives, suffering, and material poverty. A young man told me, "Everything in

Haiti is broken, except for the spirit of the Haitian people." How true.

The day before we were going to leave, one of the ladies on our team went to a store in the center of town to pick up some earrings that she had commissioned. The man in the shop told her he would not be done with the work until the next morning, but that was when we were scheduled to leave. "How am I going to get back here and pay for them in time?" she said.

One of our Haitian interpreters said that he lived nearby, and if she would give him the $100, he would stop by in the morning, pay for them, and walk them to the hotel before we left. Now you can imagine what we all thought of this. Somehow though, we were assured that he would do what he said, and the woman entrusted him with the $100. Sure enough the next morning the young man showed up, just as he said, with her earrings. We were really amazed.

"I would never take your money." The young Haitian man told us, "It's not mine."

You can see why I have said that the Haitian people were special. They were different than the people I had met in Jamaica, Mexico or the other Caribbean countries I had visited. I felt a connection to them in some place deep within me. I was intrigued by their spirit, their ability to find joy in life beyond pain, suffering, and the lack of 'things.' They seemed to have discovered some sort of secret for living. They seemed to have a pearl of great price, which I was curious to learn more about. This realization crystallized for me when I arrived back in the Miami Airport and stopped into the restroom. There I heard the sound of a father yelling at his small child who was crying and very upset. It was so painful and disturbing to listen to this. This was a sound that I had not heard all week while in Haiti, the poorest country in the Western Hemisphere. But I heard this sad and painful sound here, in the richest country.

Traditional Haitian tap-tap.

3
The Letter

Kreyòl pale, Kreyòl komprann.

Creole spoken is Creole understood.

When you have had a new experience, it is difficult to talk to people about it. There is a change in you, but to describe it with words is inadequate. I won't be able to write about it here very well either. It's like trying to describe the color green to someone born blind. It is the same problem that scientists have when trying to explain the existence of 'dark matter.' They have found that ninety-five percent of the universe is made up of dark matter, but you cannot see it or measure it. The only way scientists can tell of its existence, is by the effect it has on the rest of the visible universe. This is the same with a new experience, the only way you can explain it is by its effect on the person. I certainly was changed by what I experienced in Haiti.

I began to question how I would act on those feelings. I had a restless energy, but what direction should I take in the future? I did agree to travel to Haiti with Jean Broyles and her medical team again, but that would be the last time. A strange series of events occurred during that first trip to Cap-Haitien that helped redirect me.

A few days before I left on that trip, I was given a letter by the chair of our parish's peace and justice committee: Andrea Sexton. I had been active with that committee, and she just left this letter for me as an F.Y.I. I really did not have time to look at it, so I read it on the plane. It talked about the Diocese of Richmond's Haiti Parish Twinning Program. The coordinators of the program, Bob and Adele DellaValle-Rauth, wanted to visit with us and discuss whether or not our parish would be interested in participating. I thought to myself, "That's interesting, here I am going to Haiti and I'm reading a letter about a Haiti twinning program. I didn't know Andrea even knew that I was going to Haiti." I had a lot on my mind heading off to Haiti and all, so I just tucked the letter away and I did not think about it much until I returned.

Upon my return, the peace and justice committee had arranged for us to meet with Bob and Adele DellaValle-Rauth about their Haiti twinning project. I discussed the letter with Andrea and she was surprised to hear that I had actually been to Haiti, "What? You just came back from Haiti!" I think was Andrea's response. She had not heard about my trip, but just thought that this Haiti program would be something I would be interested in. A twinning project involves building a relationship with a parish community in Haiti, and in that way being in solidarity with the Haitian people there. This sounded like the direction I should be thinking about for future Haiti projects.

The moment I walked into that meeting and met Bob and Adele, we seemed to be in perfect synch. They understood my experience, and I think I acted somewhat manic showing off pictures and rattling off stories. I hope I did not frighten anyone, because I must have looked like a madman at the time. The bond of respect was immediate. We did not even have to say anything more. Their approach to working with the Haitian people was the same as the conclusions I was coming to. They stressed forming a relationship and getting to know the community before jumping in and helping them or doing something. I remember them saying that it was more about 'being than doing.' That statement was a bit cosmic, but I got the idea and I had to agree. Haiti was definitely a place that was different than anyplace I had seen before, and I needed to understand it better. It was refreshing to talk of my experience with people who understood and had similar experiences with the Haitian people: their warmth, their sincerity, and their sense of community. We agreed to follow up with Bob and Adele, meanwhile they would start the process of finding us a twin down in Haiti.

Now Bob and Adele are a unique couple, and the story regarding their work in Haiti, and how the Richmond Diocese Haiti Twinning program started is worth telling. It begins with Sister Rose Gallagher and Sister Frankie Barber who were in the same religious community as Sister Adele DellaValle: The Sisters of the Holy Names of Jesus and Mary. In 1980 Sr. Rose had the idea of working with Appalachian migrant workers in a town in Southwest Virginia called Chilhowie. Most of these migrants could be found in a particular apple orchard owned by the Bonham Brothers. The Sisters describe these camps as horrible and otherworldly, with murders, worker abuse, and substandard living conditions. Many of the men were alcoholics, loners, or even wandering professionals. They were ethnically black, white, or Hispanic.

About the time the Sisters started this work, groups of Haitian boat people were escaping Haiti and secretly entering Florida. If they made it into the country, they would try to survive by being employed within the 'hidden' or 'underground' economy; jobs such as migrant farm work. In the Bonham Brothers camps, the workers were not being paid regularly. They were given scraps of food to eat, or the leftovers from butchering, and made to sleep on buses or huts without heat or water.

One October, a group of Haitian migrant workers showed up, and the Sisters immediately saw that these men stood out: they were joyous amid the misery. Even though they were living in the same substandard conditions, they would be found singing, telling stories, playing dominoes, and seemingly making the best of their conditions. They did however miss their wives and children back in Haiti, and were cold and hungry.

One of the most common handicaps for these Haitian migrant workers was that they could not speak English. Sr. Rose and company decided to open a school near Chilhowie to teach these men English. Their language was Haitian Kreyòl, and they were getting cheated on their wages without even knowing it. Also, being in the country without papers, they were at the mercy of their crew leaders and the owners; Sr. Adele wanted to help them. She was able to secretly gather papers showing the abuse of these Haitian workers, and then working with a Roanoke Legal Aid Society lawyer named Greg Schell; Sr. Adele brought the whole affair to court. She fought for them, finally testifying in front of the U.S. House of Representatives sub-committee on Labor Relations, winning a settlement for the back pay of these Haitian men.

That was good news and bad news, because these Haitians were still trapped in this migrant camp, and would have to work for the people they just forced a settlement on. One of the Haitian men named Philogene Israel asked Sr. Adele if she would help him and a few other Haitian men leave the camp. As Adele put it, "How could we not help Israel escape bondage?"

Secretly one night, Israel and a group of seven other Haitian men, met the Sisters under a designated tree. It was dark, and the van doors would not even close, but they made it out to freedom. That was great, until Sr. Adele realized she had eight Haitian men with nowhere to live. So in desperation she called an old friend, Father Tom Caroluzza who was pastor of Our Lady of Nazareth (O.L.N.) in Roanoke. Fr. Caroluzza told Sr. Adele, "I'm having a potluck dinner at the church tonight, just bring them over, and I'll assign them to some of my parishioners." So the Haitians came to the potluck, ate, and afterwards Fr. Caroluzza assigned them to families, sending them off two-by-two. Sr. Adele recounts seeing a rainbow appear in the sky as they went off: a final blessing she thought.

Well this was fine for a few days, but then the parishioners started asking what Fr. Tom's long-term plan was, to which he did not really have an answer. Then he said, "Look, I have a common room in the rectory, I'll just put them up with me." They stayed with him for three to four months while Sr. Adele helped find them jobs, and other living situations in Roanoke.

During their stay, Fr. Caroluzza cooked good Italian pasta for all of them each day, until finally one evening he came home and the Haitian men told him, "No more Fr. Tom. From now on we cook for you." And they did, and he tells me it was wonderful. Fr. Tom remembers how faithful these men were to their families, sending money, and communicating by cassette tapes. They would cherish these tapes from home so much, that they would sleep with them under their pillows at night. As each of these men were placed into jobs, and the resettlement phase wound down, Sr. Adele applied for the job of Minister of Social Justice at Fr. Caroluzza's Parish: O.L.N. Most of these men are still living in the Roanoke area, and they still fondly call her 'Mummy Del.'

Another key leader, who pushed forward the awareness of Haiti in Virginia, is Bishop Walter F. Sullivan. In 1980 Bishop Sullivan was deeply affected by the news of the assassination of Bishop Oscar Romero of San Salvador. Bishop Romero had taken up the cause of the oppressed in Central America. He was moved by Bishop Romero's sacrifice, and wondered if he was doing enough as the Shepherd of his flock to help people in the third world. Bishop Sullivan then 'adopted' a Haitian child, and later was invited to Haiti by Bishop Leonard LaRoche of the Diocese of Hinche. Brother Cosmas Rubencamp went to Haiti to lay the foundation for a Diocesan project. Then in 1984 it was official that the Diocese of Richmond and Hinche were twinned, the first relationship was between the two respective Cathedrals.

Bishop Sullivan appointed Sr. Cora Marie Billings to coordinate 'Haiti Immersion Retreats' three times per year, but by the 1990's the program had grown beyond its volunteers. Sr. Adele, now Adele DellaValle-Rauth after her marriage to the social activist Bob Rauth, was asked to apply for the job. Adele was hired in 1996, and she and Bob built a strong program based on mutual understanding, visits, and solidarity. It was at this time that we met.

The more I learned about the twinning program and its philosophy, the more excited I became. I was eager to get started, but it took over a year before Bob and Adele were able to find a twin that was the right fit for us. They kept a lookout for a possible twin during their many trips. Finally, while they were in Haiti leading a group around Hinche up in the Central Plateau, a priest she had met in the past came up to her with his big smile and basso voice and said, "Adele, I want you to find me a twin." The priest was Pè Polinice Daisma, the pastor of Saint Gabriel's Church in Lascahobas Haiti, and he already had his twinning questionnaire filled out and ready to give her. Adele was somewhat surprised to see him since he was from Lascahobas, and to get to Hinche is a difficult three-hour drive over a mountain road. "I heard you were here and I tracked you down." Pol told her with a deep laugh.

He was so persistent and gracious about his desire that Adele could not say no. She knew at once who to match him up with. "I think I have a twin for you Pè Pol. Let me check it out when I get back." He was so excited; and told Adele that he would pray that she would find him a twin.

When Adele came back she told us the story about finding Pè Pol in Lascahobas as a twin for our parish. This was great news, but we had no easy way to contact him. The infrastructure in Haiti is lacking; there was no phone or Internet at the parish. There is no reliable mail service outside Port-au-Prince; most news is hand delivered. People are amazed by this, and just assume that mail and phone are everywhere: not in Haiti. We were powerless to get instant communication, so we wrote Pol a letter and had it hand carried to him, and then waited for a reply. It was like sending a probe to Mars and waiting for the photos to be sent back. Haiti, like Mars, is a distant and inaccessible place. So we waited expectantly for a response.

Several months later this raggedy, soiled envelope came to us; it looked like it had been hand carried all over Haiti (and it probably was). It was from Pè Pol! I opened it and read it with the same anticipation and excitement as those NASA scientists who were looking for those first photos from Mars to appear.

PAROISSE ST. GABRIEL
L A S C A H O B A S
c/o Missionnaires de Scheut
Port-au-Prince, Haiti

September 2, 1997
Our Lady of Perpetual Help
Salem, VA 24153 USA

Dear Tom:

The pleasure is mine to make friends with the parishioners of Our Lady of Perpetual Help. Peace and all good!

My name is Rev. Polinice Daisma, Roman Catholic Priest. I am a native Haitian born priest. I have been ordained for the Diocese of Hinche on September 23, 1984. Since 1992 I am pastor at St Gabriel Parish of Lascahobas.

St. Gabriel Parish is an old Parish. It has been founded in 1874, about 123 years ago. It is a big parish with 10 [chapels]

and more that 40,000 people. The different chapels or missions are all of them located in the rural areas very far from the parish center; these [include]:

- Sacre Coeur (Sacred Heart) of Cabestor
- St Joseph of Roche-Mulatre
- St Michael of Morne Michel

St. Gabriel is a very poor parish which [has] been a mission church long time ago. I am the second Haitian Priest to be in charge [of] this parish since its foundation.

The people of Lascahobas are struggling to survive. They have absolutely nothing: no work, no good schools for the poorest of the poor, no hospital, and no social-economic progress. At a pastoral level we have [over ten] catholic groups and movements.

We have three catholic schools in the rural areas with more than 300 children and ten teachers. We have also a Center for women promotion. The church in Lascahobas is the social service agency for the people. It provides some times for foods, clothes, health care, and it educates the majority of them.

We have tried long time ago to find a twin parish for Lascahobas. Now, I am very proud to have Our Lady of Perpetual Help as Parish sister. Thank you very much for your friendship. I will never forget it. I hope to be able to keep this relationship for a long time. I very appreciated your kind letter full of love as well as the map of your parish. I was deeply moved when I saw in the map the name of lay leaders from your parish involved in Pastoral activities.

I will be very glad to welcome you at St. Gabriel Church of Lascahobas. I would like to meet you personally even if I don't know when. It is my plan to visit with you and share the pastoral experiences of the both communities. I would like to express my sincere gratitude to dear Father Gregory for his wonderful welcome and friendly concern. I see he is a really young priest, full of fire and love. Thanks be to God. I would like to express my gratitude to all of you at the parish.

As far as help, we need to [be] able to support our schools to provide a better service to the children from the rural places. For the ones who are interested in coming on future trips, let them know that they are already welcome.

I pray that you may be filled by every graces and blessing from God. With every good wishes, I am sincerely yours in Christ,

Father Polinice Daisma
Pastor, St. Gabriel Parish, Lascahobas.

What a beautiful letter. It was so filled with welcome and love and hope. I was overcome with emotion when I read it to the parish, and that public reading was a powerful moment. People were silent and obviously moved. We are so accustomed to quick correspondence, that we often take communication for granted. Here was a letter from a man we have been trying to contact for months, but were unable to reach him until now. Rarely in my lifetime had one letter carried so much weight and promise as this one did. It reminded me of letters from long ago, when time and care was taken both in the writing and in the reading, like from Civil War soldiers to their loved ones back home. Reading it to our congregation reminded me of Paul's letters to his communities such as in Corinth, and I wondered how powerful that experience must have been for them back then. How we have lost the power of the written word in long distance human contact because of our instant and worldwide information superhighways. Now, however, with this letter, the courtship between our communities had begun.

Pè Pol typing at his desk, St. Gabriel's Parish.

4
Visitation House

Ti chen gen fos devan kay mèt li.

The little dog is always brave in front of his master's house.

I finally had a purpose, and that was to have no purpose. What I mean is that I needed to put aside my agenda, my medical bag, and return to Haiti bringing only who I am as a person and then find out who the Haitians are as a people. I wanted to get back to Haiti, and I heard that a group from Church of the Redeemer in Mechanicsville Virginia had a trip scheduled to Lascahobas in a few months. They were twinned with a women's cooperative there. I called their coordinator Sheryl Burrell; and we arranged to meet up in Miami to share transportation and accommodations in Haiti. Basically I hitchhiked along with them.

An announcement was made at our parish, and a campaign was organized to collect notebooks and pens for the kids in the Haitian school Pè Pol had written us about. Due to the parish's overwhelming generosity, I soon had a large, fairly heavy box to haul down with me. My trip to Miami, as is usual with travel, went awry. I had no way of contacting Sheryl and the group in Miami to tell them that my connection fell through, and so they went to Haiti without me, wondering who or where I was.

I arrived late in Miami and spent the night there hauling my big box of school supplies to the hotel the airline put me up in. The hotel, although near the airport, was run down, and definitely not a 'branded' chain. I was picked up in an unmarked van flying duel American flags and checked in at the window which had two inch thick bullet-proof glass on it, both ominous signs. Still dragging my big cardboard albatross to the room, I passed the bar, which was filled with loud music, and wild Latino patrons. I thought, "OK go ahead and kill the white guy dragging the box and get it over with." I decided just to scoot by and hope that they didn't notice me. All went well, and I was able to get a message to Visitation House in Port-au-Prince, where the group was staying, to tell them that I would arrive in the morning.

Waiting at the Miami Airport for the Port-au-Prince flight is always an interesting experience. There are the Haitians returning with large amounts of goods bought in the U.S. There are also, almost always, mission groups from U.S. churches going to Haiti for a project similar to my past medical trips. I often wondered whether these church groups are a welcomed sight, or a disparaging sign to the Haitians reminding them that their country needs help from the outside. I have never experienced anything but welcome from Haitians when they find out we are trying to work with their people.

For some reason on this trip, the U.S. State Department made a ruling that, 'No boxes are allowed into Haiti.' Enter once again, my box of supplies. Luckily an enterprising Haitian was at the airport with bags to sell. We forced the stuff into the biggest bag he had, but still it needed duct tape to close it. The bag did make it onto the plane, but that was the last time I saw my school supplies. I am sure someone set up a nice little market in Haiti once they got those supplies; just another donation for the cause.

The first thing that hit me when I got off the plane in Haiti was the heat. Then I saw the Port-au-Prince airport, which at the time was a mess. The grassy area in between the runways was littered with archaic, broken and abandoned planes and parts. Inside very little was working; there were several holes in the walls to the outside. One of these holes had a large, broken air conditioning unit dripping water onto a faded mural of Haitian life. A 1950's style rotary phone sat next to the 'out of order' bathroom, and I really did not notice any order to the place.

After filing for my missing box, I followed the flow of the crowd out. A Haitian man had come up to me and asked if I was Tom. He told me that Thimothè (pronounced: Tea-moe-tay) was waiting for me outside. I had heard of Thimothè; he is the young Haitian man contracted by the Diocese to chauffer all of the twinning groups that come to Haiti.

Getting out of the airport was a hurdle. The closer I came to the one exit door, the more crowded it became, with people pushing and trying to get ahead of me. Once out of the door I went onto a sidewalk lined with a tall, loose, chain link security fence packed with people on the other side yelling and asking for things in Kreyòl, most of which was unintelligible to me. Their hands and arms were reaching through the fence trying to grab at me as I made my way through the gauntlet. Once past the fence, I was funneled into the sea of people waiting outside, this made the heat even muggier. Many of the Haitian men came up to me grabbing my bags saying, "I'm with you. I'm security for you." or, "Taxi, need taxi." in broken English. I tried to be gentle but direct and finally made it to the street where I saw a man waving for me: must be Thimothè.

Thimothè was a thin, polite, quiet young man who had learned some English. He welcomed me with a big smile and said, "You must be Tom. The group wondered where you were."

"I was held up in Miami overnight. Boy, I'm glad to see you. Thanks for waiting for me Thimothè." We then traveled through Port-au-Prince to Kay Vizitasyon, or Visitation House: a Haitian guesthouse. The streets of Port-au-Prince appeared much the same as they had in Cap-Haitien, but on a larger scale, and much busier.

Driving the streets was a bit of a free-for-all void of rules other than: the bigger you are the more right of way you have, and if in doubt honk your horn and accelerate. There were the ubiquitous tap-taps, brightly colored, covered, pick-up trucks, which serve as mass transportation for the people. I had seen them in Cap-Haitien. They are privately owned, and each one has a saying painted in Kreyòl on them such as, 'God Saves,' or 'Strong Faith,' or 'Look what God has done.' Actually, they are very efficient and cheap, but crowded; there is always room for one more on a tap-tap.

We saw the usual street side vendors and people walking, lots of cars and pollution from heavy diesel smoke. There were many cinder block structures lining the route in various stages of construction. Thimothè explained that with inflation so high, it is more economical to take some money and put it into construction materials, even if you cannot finish the job. Otherwise the price of the project keeps growing out of reach. Finally we turned off Delmas 33 onto Rue A. Martial and arrived at Kay Vizitasyon.

"So there's Tom Fame!" Sheryl said, as we were welcomed on the gated circle drive outside the guesthouse. "We weren't sure that you actually existed when you didn't show up in Miami."

"Long story." I said.

As Thimothè helped with the bags, I was met by our host at Visitation House: Ron Voss. "Well, well, so the elusive Tom Fame finally arrives. Welcome to Visitation House and Haiti."

"Glad to finally get here." I said.

"Let's get you settled upstairs in a room, and then I'd like to take you all out on the soccer field to tell the story of what I have called 'The Haitian Stations of the Cross.'" Ron said, as he directed me through the house.

I was led into the large white cement house through a tiled sitting room. Past the entrance was an open communal dining area, a chapel room, and another room set up to sell crafts made by the artisans living in Cite Soleil: Haiti's poorest slum. The guest rooms looked similar to summer camp cottages, and were situated on top of the patio-like roof. They could easily accommodate large groups. Visitation House had been a private home owned by a Haitian businessman named Antwan Izmery. He was a friend of Ron's who was assassinated during the early years of Jean Bertrand Aristide's exile; Ron has run his ministries on the campus in and around this house ever since.

Ron was a tall thin man with tanned somewhat weathered skin from his years working under the Haitian sun. His bright blue eyes and light-colored hair topped a welcoming smile, which was always waiting for you when you arrived. Ron Voss is Kay Vizitasyon, and both the guesthouse and his ministries grew out of his involvement in, and witness to, some of the tumultuous events in the recent history of Haiti. I would get to know him and this house well over my many trips to Haiti.

Ron uses Visitation House itself primarily as a guesthouse, which serves as a comfortable but basic place for groups to stay when coming to work in Haiti. Next-door is Park Izmery with its soccer field, basketball courts and lawn used for boys' organized sports. Across the street he has helped a neighbor woman named Emanuella begin a local health clinic; she is also the Visitation House cook. Across from Emanuella's house is the headquarters for Pax Christi Haiti, and home to Bertony Domond or 'Domo,' a Haitian man who is Ron's right hand man for just about everything.

From the rooftop patio, I could see Park Izmery, a walled green grassy soccer oasis where Haitian boys can escape the harshness of the Port-au-Prince streets for some good hard play. I could also see the mural of The Haitian Stations of the Cross painted on the side of the far wall; this is where we were told to meet in the next hour to hear Ron tell about Haitian history.

After getting settled in, and grabbing a cool Prestige Beer, Ron sat us down on the soccer field in front of the mural of the Haitian Stations of the Cross and told us the History of Haiti. It is a history that most Americans, and sadly with the lack of education, most Haitians do not know. This is what we heard:

Haiti celebrates the 200th anniversary of its independence on New Year's Day 2004. The date: January 1, 1804, and the story of Haitian independence is one of the great stories in the proud history of the Haitian people, and for all free people in the world. But how many of us are aware of this story? A Haitian proverb states: "If you want to know a people you must know their history, and if you want to know a person you must know their family." What is Haiti's story? Why is it significant? And what has happened to Haiti since 1804?

Haiti occupies the western third of the island of Hispaniola, originally discovered by Christopher Columbus who called it 'The Pearl of the Antilles.' Haiti became a French colony that imported thousands of African slaves to work the sugar, cotton, coffee, and indigo plantations. In 1791, former slaves Jean-Jacque Dessalines, Henry Christoff, and Toussaint Louverture, lead a revolt of 400,000 fellow Africans turned Haitian slaves. Finally on New Year's Day 1804 they defeated Napoleon's French Army, considered at the time one of the premier forces in the world. Haiti, and all of its former slaves were free; the first and only time in the history of civilization that an enslaved people freed themselves from their captors.

Toussaint Louverture went on to write their constitution and opened Haiti to all people fleeing slavery. The fighting was so devastating to France both militarily and economically, that in 1803 Napoleon gave up his aspirations for a French colony in Louisiana. Napoleon sold the Louisiana Territory to President Jefferson so that Napoleon could help fund his army, which was busy with the French revolution. That is how the U.S. acquired one of the biggest pieces of land that now makes up our country. Haitians also fought alongside U.S. revolutionary soldiers at the battle of Savannah during our fight for independence.

Haiti, as an independent nation of freed slaves that welcomed others fleeing slavery, did not sit well with President Jefferson. Jefferson himself had slaves, so Haiti was not recognized by the United States until after the Civil War. France also refused to recognize Haiti until they paid France for their 'economic losses,' that is the price of the slaves. In 1825, Haiti was coerced into paying 90 million gold francs ($21 billion U.S. today) as reparation for the cost of all the 'human property' France had lost. This debt took 100 years for Haiti to pay off, and was accomplished by closing Haiti's public schools, and by selling off their great wealth of tropical hardwood forests. This hardwood clear cutting decimated Haiti, which is about 90% deforested today.

The U.S. invaded and occupied Haiti from 1915 to 1932 to protect and secure U.S. and European interests. Unfortunately, the security forces that our country trained and left behind later became the Haitian Army, the strong-arm tool of all the dictators to follow. These included Francois 'Papa-Doc' Duvalier and his son Jean-Claude.

In 1986 Jean-Claude 'Baby-Doc' Duvalier fled Haiti with $700 million of his country's money to the protection of France. A voice of a small Catholic priest, Jean-Bertrand Aristide, from the poor Haitian parish of St. Jean Bosco, began to excite the people to resist the fear of the Army. This led to Aristide's election as president in 1990, the first time in the history of Haiti that power had changed hands peacefully, and the first time Haitians had voted. Haiti's recent move to democracy has been turbulent. After only one year in office, Aristide was exiled by a coup in 1991 and then finally returned with great jubilation in 1994. Aristide only served two and a half years of his five-year term.

Ron went on to tell us, "The events that forced the end of the Duvalier rule and then the first free election of President Aristide, made for very turbulent times. I have known and witnessed many martyrs and much suffering of the Haitian people. I have put these names and events together into a prayerful remembrance that I have called The Haitian Stations of the Cross, or Chemen Kwa P'ep Ayisyen. I'll go through them with you as illustrated on the mural. I also take groups through Port-au-Prince and I can show you the actual places." Ron went on to recount these stories:

Station 1: Saint Jean Bosco Church, Father Aristide's parish where he preached for an end to dictatorship. When he refused to stop preaching, the Tonton Macoute military came into the congregation with machetes and massacred the people. They then torched the church, which lies burnt today. That was September 11, 1988.

Station 2: Cite Soleil, the poorest and most desperate slum in our Hemisphere, besides the poverty and filth, many people had been killed here while demanding aid.

Station 3: Fort Dimanche was the infamous 'torture prison' of the Duvaliers. It was reopened after Aristide's exile. The people had such a hatred for this place, that upon Aristide's return they demolished it by hand, block by block, using the material for houses that still stand in Cite Soleil today.

Station 4: Takes us to the waterfront and to Port-au-Prince's major port facility. We remember that the seaport is the main doorway to economic and military control. The water is also what separates and locks the Haitian people in, many of whom have died at sea trying to flee their poverty.

Station 5: The American Embassy is a symbol of the interwoven history and relationship between our two countries over the years.

Station 6: Commemorates the last massacre of the Haitian people during the coup d'etat years. On September 30, 1994 hundreds of thousands of Haitians attended Mass at the cathedral, and then marched to the National Cemetery to 'bury the coup' in a ceremonial protest. The slaughter that ensued led to international outrage and a return for Aristide that year.

Station 7: The National Palace or 'White House' has been the seat of Haitian power, and had turned into a symbol of hope with the peaceful transition of power from Aristide to Renè Prèval in 1996.

Station 8: The former military headquarters building, the center of oppression for the Haitian people, now houses the headquarters for The Ministry of Women's Conditions.

Station 9: The Man of Peace statue outside of the National Palace is dedicated to all who gave their lives during the years of transition to democracy. We also recognize the 'Nèg Mawon' statue, The Wild Man, who is blowing the lambi shell signaling Haiti's freedom in 1804.

Station 10: The Catholic Cathedral of Notre Dame is a symbol of the important role that the Catholic Church has played in the social network of the Haitian people.

Station 11: Sacre Coeur Church is where Antwan Izmery was pulled out onto the street and shot in the head just for speaking about Aristide on the fifth anniversary of the massacre at St. John Bosco church: September 11, 1993. His brother George, also a local businessman, was later killed. Antwan Izmery's former home now serves as Visitation House and its ministries.

Station 12: The spot near Sacre Coeur where Guy Mallory, the Minister of Justice, was also gunned down for speaking out against the coup. This was a time of severe hopelessness for the Haitian people.

Station 13: The front gate of the home for the Montfort priests. This is the spot where Father Jean Marie Vincent is buried. He was one of Haiti's most popular priests and earliest peasant organizer; we remember his works and sacrifice after being brutally murdered on August 28, 1994.

Station 14: La Famni Selavi, Father Aristide's orphanage that had been destroyed several times, but now serves as a source of hope for all the girls and boys it ministers to.

"We end with this symbol of resurrection, the orphanage, because as people of faith, the Haitian people are also people of hope." Ron would say, and then we would end with a prayer, a song to the Holy Spirit: "O Lespri Sen."

Over the years I would get to know Ron Voss and see him work with the Haitian people. Ron helped many groups get in and out of Haiti, and facilitated their ministries. He recounted his story of The Haitian Stations of the Cross hundreds and hundreds of times, as he helped many groups of Americans understand Haiti. He often appeared melancholy as he suffered alongside his Haitian friends, and struggled with his own personal demons. He endured several incidences of being held at gunpoint; a feeling he would describe as profound victimization. After one of these events he told me that he cried for 45-minutes feeling so helpless. Ron Voss is a man who understood Peter's words, "By his wounds you have been healed."

Thimothè Samuel.

Ron Voss speaking to a group at the mural of
The Haitian Stations of the Cross.

Park Izmery, Port-au-Prince, Haiti.

5
Pè Pol

Sonje lapli ki leve mayi ou.

Remember the rain that made your corn grow.

The sun comes up early in Haiti, not just because you are further south, but because of all the morning activity and noises out on the street. Throughout the night there are the cat fights, the dogs barking, the roosters crowing, and then the trucks start grrrring and honking. People get up very early to walk to work or to market in order to beat the hot sun. For this reason people can be heard early on walking and talking. I could hear the tinkling of small bells, usually from someone walking by and signaling a service such as a shoeshine. I have even heard the megaphoned street preacher try to save an early morning soul. So morning came early in Haiti the day we got ready to ride to Lascahobas.

Sheryl and the group from Church of the Redeemer were downstairs taking in their cups of coffee, which Ron had prepared for us. "Thimothè should be here after we eat, so just pile your bags out on the drive for him." Sheryl told us.

All five of us fit into Thimothè's S.U.V. and we headed out of Port-au-Prince. It was already getting hot, so the breeze through the open car windows felt good. The usual traffic seemed to become less dense as we headed towards the outskirts of the city, until we came to Croix des Bouquets the last transportation hub out of town. The main intersection was densely packed with sellers and buyers, buses and tap-taps, people and more people all dodging in and out between moving vehicles. With the traffic slowed down by the congestion, kids would come up to the car windows selling drinks, candy or phone cards. In the middle of this busy intersection, I could barely make out the raised triangular flower garden with a large white crucifix standing in it for which this suburb was named. The cross was lost now in the busyness of people, vehicles, and commerce.

Once out of the Port-au-Prince metropolitan area, we started picking up some speed on a one-and-a-half lane paved road that seemed to head straight and flat out of town towards the mountains. Soon the pavement ended onto a dusty dirt road in the countryside with cactus, scrub brush and desert-like dirt; it looked like Arizona. There were no trees to be seen on this desert plane, or on the approaching mountain: Mon Kabrit (Goat Mountain). These mountains reminded me of ones that I'd seen in New Mexico, and Thimothè told us that a long time ago they were covered with tropical rain forests and birds, all lost to the early deforestation. We could see our mountain road with its eroded edges all the way up along the side as it climbed. Travel slowed significantly once we hit that dirt road, but especially climbing Mon Kabrit. Amazingly, this is Haiti's National Highway #3.

This mountain road was not made for those with a fear of heights; when I looked out the side window I had the sense of flying. The narrow road climbed very high up overlooking the desert plane below with no guardrails. It was littered with shells of abandoned and overturned vehicles on and over the road. Traffic was not heavy, but there were large trucks filled with produce, and people riding way up on top of them. It was tense enough passing them on those narrow mountain roads, but that was nothing compared with the concern I had watching those Haitians holding on, atop the truck while being rocked from side to side. People are known to fall off of these kamyons (pronounced ka-me-owns) on occasion.

The entire route to Mirebalais was windy, dusty, very bumpy, and slow due to the rocks and road ditches. Wherever there was a slow spot or a turn, you would find a child or an older women looking hungry and dirty asking for some spare change. We passed through a small village called Terre Rouge at one of the narrow mountain passes. It was a place where all of the drivers stopped for food bought at the roadside stands and the route was littered with used Styrofoam plates.

From Terre Rouge we started descending slowly towards Mirebalais, as we did you could see the mountains rolling into the distance, and seeming to extend on forever. Both the mountains and the roadside terrain started to look greener but not lush by any account.

Mirebalais is a good-sized village, a center of transportation and commerce. We stopped at St. Louis' Church rectory on the town square for a rest and some water. It was market day, and the large central town square was lined with vendors selling things alongside the wrought iron park fence.

While Sheryl's group waited in the rectory, I wanted to go out onto the street and walk around the market. Most of the locals tried to appear as if they were ignoring me, but I could tell they were all staring and talking after I passed. I stopped at a spot where a man was selling an assortment of straw hats and I thought, "With this sun, I could really use one of those."

So I stopped and picked one out and was trying to find out how much it was when a Haitian man who had lived in the U.S. came to my aid, "That would be about 100 goudes. You can give him $3.00 U.S."

"Thanks." I said, and we had a nice little conversation about who he was, and what we were doing in Haiti. Talking with this Haitian man made others feel more comfortable, and soon my hat purchase was the biggest show on the square.

When I turned around I noticed that a large crowd of spectators had gathered behind me. I said, "Bonjou." to the newly formed crowd, returned to the rectory, and then we headed out of town.

Mirebalais is a crossroads in the Central Plateau; it's the main stop from Port-au-Prince, and once out of town you could go either north to Hinche or east to Lascahobas and then onto the Dominican Republic. The road to Lascahobas was relatively flat, and for the first time I felt like I was in the tropics. The route was lined with trees and vegetation occasionally hanging over the road creating some shade. The valley and the mountains along the route were beautiful and green; the road was lined by family farm-fields with banana and coconut trees, beans and corn, and other crops. This was very lush country.

Even though we were out in the country, the road had almost constant foot traffic; women coming and going to market, men coming and going to their fields, and children in school uniforms or carrying water. It had a much more peaceful feel than the city, and much more life than the desert area on Mon Kabrit. I was feeling at peace with this place.

Sixty miles and three and a half hours later, we came to an old narrow, rusting steel bridge, and Thimothè told us, "This is the Lascahobas River, we're coming to town."

As we crossed over, women could be seen on the side of the river washing clothes against the rocks, beside them a multicolored patchwork of drying clothes was laid out on the ground sunning. We were relieved when our vehicle climbed up onto the street paving stones, and the ride became smooth, I hadn't realized how much work it was to ride your seat along that bumpy road: like being on a three-hour bull-ride.

Lascahobas was a nice village, smaller than Mirebalais, and less busy and hurried. The street was lined by small cinderblock homes and offices, and the streets led to a central grassy square fronted by the large white face of Saint Gabriel's Church with its bell tower. It was impressive for the size of the village. A quick stop at the parish told us that Pè Pol was away on business, and that he was expecting us later.

Sheryl and the group were meeting with Josette from the Lambi Foundation; they work with Bernadette and the other women in a Lascahobas cooperative called A.F.A.L. (Asosyasyon Fanm Activ Laskawobas). I tagged along, and Josette told us all about how Lambi was started, and how it worked to empower women to create a better economic environment for their children and families through micro-loans and training.

The lambi is a great Haitian symbol of freedom; it is represented by the Nèg Mawon statue near the National Palace. When the slaves would break free of their chains and their master's house, they would run off into the mountains and hide; they were called wild men, in Kreyòl 'nèg mawon.' Once free they would blow a conch shell: the lambi. The sound of the lambi not only brought the escaped slaves together, it was a signal of hope to those who were still enslaved that freedom was near.

Bernadette was a very welcoming and gracious host. After Josette's presentation, Bernadette brought us into the A.F.A.L. meeting room where she had prepared food for us. It was my first taste of real Haitian food, she served bouyon: a spicy soup-stew that was wonderful. Sheryl and company would be staying with Bernadette, and I would be with Pè Pol at the rectory. We would see each other in passing, but they would be going back to Port-au-Prince without me in a few days. I said good-bye, and walked back to the rectory to finally meet Pè Pol.

It was just a short walk down the street to the church grounds; a high cement wall surrounded the rectory complex. I could see the arches, which formed the second floor of the rectory, rising above the wall. Passing through a metal gate I entered into a grassy area with some gardens. It was a pleasant space surrounded on three sides by the workers quarters and kitchen, the back of the church, and the rectory. A woman was sitting just outside the doorway to the kitchen area beating something in a large bowl, I waved hello to her and said, "Bon swa." She smiled back and then I heard Pol's voice.

"Tom. Welcome my friend." Pol said with a big welcoming smile and arms outstretched to embrace me. He is a tall man, perhaps six foot, with a deep basso voice that always had a hint of laughter to it. He knew some English, which was a big relief because I did not know any Kreyòl or French.

I walked towards Pol as he was coming from the rectory, I gave him a big hug and said, "Bon swa Pè Pol, it's great to finally be here." While holding each other's forearms, we just looked at each other and smiled. We then talked briefly about my travels; he asked about my family, and how everyone was at the parish, and then he introduced me to Pè Jethro, his assistant priest.

"Welcome." Pol said again leading me towards the rectory, "Know that you are home now, this house is your house. Come, I'll show you your room, you can get situated and then we have fixed some food for you." We stepped into the rectory and all I could think of was how much Bouyon I had already eaten at Bernadette's. Being a gracious guest in Haiti can be filling.

Entering the rectory, I saw a great communal dining room, with high ceilings, a pantry, and a large table in the center. The walls were brightly painted and decorated with paper flowers, and hand written signs saying 'Bonne Fette' and 'Bonne Anne' in preparation for the coming New Year's celebration. Pol opened the refrigerator, which was cold only because a large piece of ice was placed on the bottom shelf,

"There is no electricity." Pol told me. "Would you like a beer?" He asked, pulling out a couple bottles of Prestige.

"Sure, thanks Pol." I accepted. We just looked at each other, and he said something about how the women had decorated the room for the New Year, and how everyone was ready for the great celebration in the church. We clinked bottles and he directed me towards the stairs.

"Come." Pol said, "I will show you your room." He led me up a tiled stairway with a large round wooden banister. The rectory was well built and comfortable looking, even without electricity. The second floor rooms were surrounded by a covered walkway with arched openings overlooking the yard and the street. He opened up a door to one of the rooms and said with his usual smiling, musical voice, "Here you are Tom, this is where you stay."

I went into a very plain room with vacant walls, and about four simple beds pushed over to one side. Against the window was one of those simple beds, freshly made up, and with a single fresh flower lying on it beside a colorful hand written sign that read:

Tom. Welcome.
You are no longer a foreigner.
You are a brother. You are at home.

It was so touching. I really had a tear or two when I saw this simple room and bed, made into the grandest room I had ever stayed in. Beautiful not because of what was there, but because of the care with which they had prepared it, and the love with which they welcomed me.

"Get some rest, and then you can come down for dinner later." Pol said. And I did get some needed rest.

We sat down for dinner with a beautifully set table, and quite a feast set out. A prayer of grace and welcoming, and we ate. Pol, Jethro, and I communicated through smiles and gestures, and their English. I found out that Pol was the second Haitian priest in this old parish that was started as a French mission in 1874. There was a photo on the wall of a Pere Blot, a Belgian Priest who was pastor for over 30 years, and built the present church, rectory, and many of the mission chapels in the countryside. All of the people who remembered Pere Blot spoke of him as a saint. Another old black and white photo showed the original rectory from the turn of the century; it was very remote and tropical looking.

After we finished, Pol wanted to show me the grounds and the church. Through the back door of the rectory was a peaceful garden courtyard, with a bird coop and some chickens. Without refrigeration, live is best until you are ready to cook them. Pol obviously had pride in his parish grounds. I could hear singing coming from the church, so we went over to visit.

The church space was large, and well constructed of decorative cinderblocks. Although it was not ornate, it had a simple beauty and dignity. There was a youth group choir practicing. Uniformed boys and girls that reminded me of boy scouts were all lined up in the first ten rows of pews. "This is Kiro." Pol told me. "They are one of many youth groups in the parish; they help with the running of the church, singing, and perform service projects to help the sick and others in need in the parish." Pol introduced me to some of the leaders, many of whom I would get to know very well over the years.

One of those leaders was a man named Venel Lamay, although not heavy, he had rounded features, a gentle and soft-spoken manner, with a bashful but engaging smile. He was very talented musically, and helped out by playing the keyboard and teaching music to many of the youth.

Venel told me that he had been recently married, and although he did not own much himself, he said, "I want to help the poor. It would not be right if I worked hard and acquired more than those people who suffer around me. I should get what I need, and if God gives me more, I should use it to help other people in town." Here is a poor man, who sees himself as needing to serve the truly poor.

While talking with Venel, I noticed someone hobbling into the church from the back. Approaching us was this bone thin, poor little girl, dirty and dressed in tattered clothes; she walked using a broken stick to support her bent limbs and back. She was the saddest girl I had seen in Haiti, "They call her Tifi." Venel told me. "She doesn't have any parents."

Tifi came up to me and touched my arm, and then took my hand in hers. She looked up into my eyes with a sad and quizzical gaze as if to say, "What is this person here?" Her eyes looked empty as if she had nothing to give, because she had never received. I stood there for a minute while she held onto my hand; then looking down and away towards the others in the church, she just dropped my hand, turned, and slowly shuffled out the back of the church, bent and leaning onto her walking stick. I had never seen anyone like her before.

Pè Pol and I sat out on the balcony that evening talking while watching the people walking along the street below. "All of those people are my parishioners." Pol said. "They rely on me for everything. Sometimes I can give it to them, and sometimes all I can do is pray for them. But we do what we can, their needs are so many." We sat for a while in silence. Finally Pol stood up to leave and said, "We'll have Mass in the morning, pass a good-night Tom."

"OK, I'll see you then." I said, and went off to bed.

The Lascahobas nights were quieter than those in Port-au-Prince, but morning still came early. "BOONNG!" I heard as I jumped up from sleep. "It's 5am!" I said, as the loud church bells continued to sound. The steeple was right across the balcony from my room. I arose and took my bucket of water to the shower station and cleaned up for Mass, there was no running water in the rectory either I found out.

After Mass, Pè Pol, Jethro, and I sat down for breakfast. We prayed together, and then shared a meal together once again. I have to say I have never eaten spaghetti for breakfast before. They seemed to be so relaxed and took their time with breakfast, even stopping to say good-morning to the few people who came by and poked their heads in the door. With all the help that Haiti needs, and that the parishioners need, I thought that they would have a very busy schedule. "What are you all planning to do today?" I asked.

Pol did not look concerned, or rushed, and replied, "Oh, we haven't got much planned. Pè Jethro is going to talk to some people, and I thought we could go visit some of the outstations."

Somehow they got things done, but were not frantic about it the way we seem to be. It was so nice to just sit and share a meal together, to take time together with each other. I remembered how the disciple's eyes were opened in the breaking of the bread. How important it is, I found out, to just take the time to share a meal. This is one of the fundamentals of building a relationship.

I went outside the front gate and stood out on the street watching the people pass by. Thimothè was sitting in his car waiting to pick up Sheryl and her group. One of the men in the group, John, was also waiting. He was a somewhat portly fifty-something year old, and we talked as people walked by. Once again I saw little Tifi on her walking stick coming our way, I thought, "Boy she can spot a blan, like a vulture can spot carrion." She shuffled up to John looking much thinner in the daylight, and I could tell he looked uncomfortable, becoming fidgety, and forming a furrowed brow. As Tifi stood next to John, staring up at him, he just stood there not knowing what to do, and hoping that she would move on. Tifi took her hand and patted his paunch, and at the same time looked up and held out her hand to him. This image struck with me as iconic, John so overweight and Tifi so emaciated, her saying in effect, "Why do you have so much, while I have so little. Can you not give me a little of what you have? Please." John became even more uncomfortable and stepped back. I just looked at Tifi with deep sorrow, and felt I had to give her something. So I knelt down and held her in my arms and cried for her. How is it that there is a human being like her on this earth?

Later, Pol called for me from within the rectory yard, "Tom, are you ready to go?"

He was going to show me around 'the zone,' and visit a rural chapel. "I'm ready to go. How far is the walk?" I asked.

Pol again put on one of his big smiles and laughed, "Ha ha. Can you ride a motorcycle?"

Village of Lascahobas, Haiti. Main Street on market day.

6
Lascahobas

Roch nan dlo pa konnen doule roch nan soley.

The rock in the water does not know the pain of the rock in the sun.

"Pol, I didn't know you had a motorcycle." I said, somewhat surprised. Then Pol signaled me to go around back with him. He was dressed in a sky-blue cotton shirt that hung below his waist. It had four front pockets with embroidered images of Haiti; palm trees, flowers, women at work, and the word 'Haiti' embroidered over the left pocket. "I like your shirt." I said.

"It's a special shirt for priests in Haiti. When we go out in the country and people see us wearing this, they will know that we are priests." Pol explained, with a sense of pride in his vocation. "Here we are." Pol said while pointing at two motorcycles. They were dirt bikes, and from the looks of them they were wearing a lot of Haitian dirt.

"Cool. Can I ride one?" I questioned.

"No. Just this one is mine, jump on." Pol instructed. He took it out, and revved it up. "JUMP ON!" Pol yelled over the loud buzz of the engine, and we were off. I was having a great time with this, and Pol was enjoying that he could give me this gift.

As we headed out of town, we passed Sheryl and company returning in Thimothè's car. They smiled and waved at us as we passed. About a mile later we left the road and entered a down sloping field with several paths leading in every direction. Pol told me to hang on; I had no idea how he knew which path to take, but he knew. I thought about how the Good Shepherd will lead you by right paths. Pol is my Shepherd today.

We were buzzing along heading generally downwards along a winding dirt walking path; wind and dust went flying past my smiling face. The sun flickered through the broad green banana leaves as we passed by. Even out here there were people everywhere, walking and working. At one point Pè Pol stopped, and yelled something in Kreyòl to a couple of young men up on a hill. After continuing on for a short distance, we came to a lake. "This is the river. We need to cross it to get to the outstations." Pol explained.

It was Lake Peligre, formed by a hydroelectric dam holding back the Artibonite River. "Wow, this is great!" I said with wide eyes and a smile. The lake was surrounded by those green, field covered Haitian mountains, which are a source of both beauty and hardship for the Haitians who have to walk them every day. The water was still and flat reflecting the blue Haitian sky; in the distance I could see a small boat making its way across. A white crane came flying by low and fast, skimming over the surface of the water before landing on a log outcropping. It was all so beautiful.

Two boys where playing in the water nearby, splashing each other, they came out to look at us when we arrived. The boys were not wearing a thing, and they did not seem the least bit bothered by this. Pè Pol seemed to know them, they talked while standing there with their shiny wet dark bodies. Seeing enough, they ran back and dove in to play.

About that time, the young men Pè Pol had talked to along the trail came paddling around the cove towards us in a large dug out canoe. After some words, they came up and loaded Pol's motorcycle onto the canoe and we got in. The canoe was fairly full with the bike, the two paddlers, and us; but they pushed off and headed for the other side. The playing boys splashed us as we left: a final blessing.

I remember thinking, "Am I really here." It felt like a scene from National Geographic.

Once out on the water it was quiet and cool. As we moved across the lake, I could see the crane push off from its perch with slow powerful strokes in flight, silhouetted by the shoreline. I just sat and looked, taking in the wonder of it all. Our rowers started singing to the rhythm of the paddles, and Pol just smiled at me and laughed, "Do you like it?"

"Yeah. It's pretty good." I replied in what was an understatement. We unloaded on the other side, and mounted the bike as Pol gave parting instructions to the boatmen. The trail led to a newly built church, the plaster was still drying. We had arrived at Our Lady of Altagrace Chapel, Pol told me. Next to the church was a very old, very large, shady tree, with a group of about 50 people underneath it praying and listening to scripture.

"The people have been meeting under this tree to pray for 50 years." Pol instructed. "We got the money to build a church and now they can have a priest to make a parish of their own."

The people were excited by the surprise visit from their pastor, and offered us a tour. The young children were scared of the blan and hid behind their mothers. I was amazed to see so many people gathered on a Tuesday morning. "All they have is their Faith." Pol said as we were taken on a tour.

Later while standing out under the great tree, a small boy came up and stared at me with an inquisitive smile. Pol told me that they do not get many outsiders here. The boy was holding a soccer ball made out of a bundle of old used white plastic shopping bags held together with twine. He even used a few black bags to give it that soccer ball look. Another small boy was using one of the same old weathered bags tied to a thread, and was flying it like a kite.

The heat of the midday tends to slow you down, and these folks were taking time together, enjoying each other's company, and the company of some visitors. This is the real Haiti, I told myself. You do not see this Haiti on the news. We stayed a few hours and then were off after Pol finished some business with the elders. At the shore, our boatmen were waiting patiently for our return trip.

When we returned to town at midday, the streets were less busy. The heat had brought people to rest; Pol and I joined them with a siesta.

That afternoon I sat in the yard with a boy about ten years old, and we played 'teach me some Kreyòl.' I drew animals and things, and he would teach me their Kreyòl names. His name is Roland; we had a good laugh when he taught me the word for snake, and then he made a wriggly snake like motion with his hand and arm, "Koulev!" he said. I jumped in mock fright and he laughed hard, repeating the action many times never tiring of my reaction. I have watched Roland grow up to be a nice young man, and still to this day whenever we meet he will make the sign of the snake with his arms and say, "Koulev!" to our laughter. It's our sign.

Later, I went out to wander the streets of Lascahobas to see what was happening; women where coming back from market and kids from school. At the police station across from the church, a few local policemen were sitting under the shade with their chairs cocked back against the wall. I heard the sound of wood and scraping coming from behind one of the buildings and went to look.

Walking through a small alley between some shops I came into an open area under a large shade tree. A man stood there with a planer and hand hued lumber on a worktable; he was planing the wood. He was a strong dark man with a soft round face, close cut hair, and wearing almost nothing except sweat and torn shorts. There were not any power tools, or power for that matter. He immediately greeted me with a broad smile broken up only by the gap between his front teeth. Excitedly he waved me in. His name is Jean-Jacques Gabriel Baptiste, but his friends call him Jean Claude. Standing there with his tools and wood, he reminded me of Joseph and his carpenter son.

Together we shared a language that only bodies can speak, and eyes can hear, but we connected. I thought Jean Claude was just making a wooden board, but he gathered some of the pieces he had been working on and loosely assembled them into a beautiful hand carved dresser.

"Wow." I said, "That's beautiful Jean Claude."

I took a photo of him doing his work and then he yelled something into his house; the whole family came out: four children and his wife. He instructed them to go back inside and motioned me to wait. When they came back, they were dressed cleanly and ready for a family photo. I could tell how proud Jean Claude was of his family, and the mutual love between him and his wife. There was an abandoned Mack dump truck on the side of the yard, and they wanted the photo taken in front of the truck.

After we finished with the photos, he then brought me a newly carved chair, and I sat and 'talked' with him and his family for about an hour. He is a gregarious man, with a gravelly voice and ever-present smile. When I got up to leave he gave me a great big 'thanks for the visit' hug. By the strength of his vice grip hug, I knew this was a man who worked with his hands.

Later, I went out into the town square and just sat there watching Lascahobas go by. Some young men stopped to practice English with me; a group of children wanted to touch and pinch my skin to see what white skin felt like. After sitting there for a while, I began to fade into the scenery. About that time I saw Tifi shuffling over with her stick. She sat next to me and looked up at me as she does; she cannot speak. Finally she curled up into a fetal position under my arm with her thumb in her mouth, and fell into a deep sleep. She must have slept for almost an hour. A relaxed, restful sleep, I wondered what she was dreaming about. How peacefully she slept, like a baby sleeps. I wondered how often, if ever, she gets to experience human touch like this. Suddenly she awoke, got up, and finally walked off. With all that she lacks, the one thing she needs most cannot be bought. She taught me much that day.

At dinner Pol and I talked with Jethro about our adventure across the lake, and Jethro was surprised that I actually enjoyed it. I guess that type of travel gets old day after day. They tried telling me a Haitian joke, and I realized that humor is very culturally dependent. I really did not get it, but meal times had become a chance for Kreyòl lessons. It's a good way to share; we all can learn and teach at the same time. Evening also brought the sounds of the choirs back as they practiced for the New Year's celebration tomorrow. Later we sat outside listening to them and talking before retiring.

Early the next morning, I went outside the gate to see the street scene. There was obviously much more foot traffic than I had ever seen before. Women with large bunches of bananas on their heads, mules loaded with goods, men with sacks of charcoal and much more. As people passed I would give them a "Bonjou." And I was surprised that even with their heavy loads; they would turn and smile, returning the greeting. I saw little Tifi walk into the clinic across the street. "Wonder what she's up to?" I thought, soon she came out with a handful of pills in her hand. “She has a way of taking care of herself.” I laughed, shaking my head.

Back in the yard I asked Pol. “Why are all the people out today?”

“It’s Wednesday: market day in Lascahobas. They’re getting food for the festival.” Pol replied. “The other big market day is Saturday. Would you like to see? The market is just down the street.”

“Yeah. Thanks.” I said, and left to follow the crowd to the market. Out on the street it really was a one way stream of people, animals, and produce all getting more and more dense heading into town towards the market area. The store buildings lining the street were open and full. There were many people with roadside stands and tables selling books, candy, shoes, and house wares. The crowd squeezed through a narrow alley between two of the shops and we entered the market bazaar.

The market was a dirt-covered yard with rows of tin-roofed shelters held up with sticks. Laid out on mats on the ground were all types of fruits, rice, fish, coffee, salt, beans, soap, and much more. It was crowded and I had to keep ducking, my 6 foot 2 inch frame was not built for this.

The ground was muddy from the evening’s rain; still the food was lying out there. The place had the smell of a garbage dump, mixed with charcoal smoke. I came to the ‘meat department’ where a whole side of beef lay hanging partially butchered, the cuts lying on a table exposed to the heat and flies. I thought to myself, “Obviously their health issues go beyond handing out blood pressure meds.” Public health has to be the primary concern here.

At the very end of the market were piles and sooty sacks of ‘chabon,’ charcoal, the main fuel source in Haiti. Many people attribute the cause of Haiti's deforestation to the cutting of trees to make charcoal. Although this is a problem, I have usually seen that the Haitian people are quite smart at only taking down old, non-producing trees. They seem to have a practical knowledge of how to use nature wisely.

As I worked my way out of the market, several curious people talked with me, and let me take their photo. I was open to talking with anyone who wanted to talk. Then this man came up to me, dressed only in 3 quarters length ripped pants, and carrying what looked like a log about as tall as he was. He seemed happy to see me; he came over and we gave each other a hug as he rambled on in rapid Kreyòl. Some men who were looking on started laughing at the scene, and with the man's torn and unkempt look, I thought, "OK, so he's poor. I'll greet and talk to anyone. People are people. He could be a Holy Fool."

He continued talking, so I smiled and nodded. Then when I had listened enough, I started walking away: but not alone. I had picked up a friend. We left the market together with his hand holding my wrist: men do that in Haiti. He was still carrying this long log over his shoulder like a rifle, and I just kept thinking, "I hope it's not some sort of weapon." He was a strong looking man.

So here we were, hand in hand, blan and talkative log carrying Haitian, together walking down the middle of the busy market day streets. I'm glad that I was able to bring some cheer to the many people watching that morning; by their laughter they seemed to be enjoying the scene.

When we came into the churchyard, Pè Pol was out talking with someone and saw us enter. "Ha Haaaaa." He laughed. "Tom. You have found a magician."

"A magician?" I thought.

“He would like to dance for you. Would you like?” Pol inquired.

Again I thought, “A dancing magician? What is this place? Yeah, sure,” I agreed. “I’d like to see him dance.”

We gave him the nod, Pol still chuckling with his deep throaty laugh, and then the man took the log off of his shoulder; I could see that it was hollow with a small hole at one end. He rested the open end of the log on the ground, and pulled out a rusty beat up 4 oz. paint can from his pocket. The can had small rocks in it which made a rattling sound when shook. Then with his mouth blowing into the log’s small hole, tuba-style, he began shaking and beating that can onto the side of the log. The man danced to a shake-n-bang fast rhythm using the can, over the slow musical base rhythm from the log. I just shook my head in disbelief: it was wonderful. This crazy man was actually playing and dancing for me, and I have to admit it was pretty cool. What a fantastic gift he gave me. I clapped and yelled once he finished, and he seemed quite proud of himself by the look of his broad smile.

“You can give him some money if you want.” Pol instructed.

So I gave him a few dollars, and with another hug he left us. I guess Pol meant to say he was a musician.

“He’s a crazy man.” Pol said

“Yeah, I figured that out Pol. Thanks for the warning.” I said with a smile, and then we laughed together. I would find several other characters like him whom I would meet again and again on future visits. Nothing or no one is hidden on the streets of Lascahobas. Yet every person can find their place.

Later that afternoon I went up the street to look at the St. Gabriel’s School Pol and I had passed on the motorcycle yesterday. The gate into the schoolyard was cracked open, and I entered. The stone courtyard had a few trees and was surrounded by two stories of classrooms on three sides. The Kiro group was meeting there; I saw Venel, one of the Kiro leaders, and we greeted each other.

"We're having a practice." Venel said, "Would you like us to give you a demonstration?"

I nodded yes, and with some whistles from the leaders, the kids all lined up sharply into patrols. More commands were given, and they stomped their feet responding together with strong voices. "Yes Sir!" With another couple of whistles they marched around the yard chanting in time. They ended up forming a square around me and started singing and clapping a beautiful song of greeting.

"Welcome, clap. Welcome, clap. Welcome to our guest, Tom, clap-clap-clap." And on and on they sang with what was obviously one of the group's traditional greetings. I was moved by this. Just another surprise, I am constantly surprised by these fantastic Haitian people.

I clapped for them in appreciation; then they all scattered and I asked Venel, "Haitians like to sing, don't they?"

Venel answered me, "Yes. We say that Haitians sing so that they will know that they are not alone." We talked some with the kids and then Venel told me, "Sister Laurette is in the school if you want to visit?" And he pointed to the office door.

No one was at the door, but it was cracked so I entered cautiously and called out, "Bon swa. Hello, is anybody here?" I entered into what looked more like the foyer to residential quarters.

I heard voices coming from downstairs. "Bon swa. Ki moun ap vini?" One of the Sisters asked, "Who is there?" Up came three Haitian nuns. "Byenveni. Welcome, I Sister Laurette." The head nun told me with a smile. "Chita. Sit."

I was directed into the greeting room where we sat and spoke, once again using gestures and Sr. Laurette's minimal English. I could gather that the Sisters ran the school, which was closed now for the holiday. After a while they directed me downstairs, they seemed to have something for me. Downstairs was their kitchen and common dining area. They sat me down at the table, took out some glasses, and poured us all a chocolate, creamy drink. By the small portions, I could tell this might have a little kick to it. We toasted, and sipped; the Sisters giggling in a high chirping laugh. It was definitely some type of chocolate liqueur, and they could tell I liked it. "Would you like?" Sister Laurette asked pointing at the bottle.

"Yes." I said. Then Sr. Laurette gave some orders to the other nuns who went upstairs. Laurette took an empty glass bottle and poured what looked like water into it from a pitcher; she rinsed it out, emptied it and went upstairs. I wondered if that old bottle was going to be clean enough by just rinsing it with water. Then I thought, "Hmmm. Just water?" I checked out the pitcher of water; it was moonshine! "Naughty Sisters!" I thought, with a laugh.

They returned with a gift-wrapped bottle of chocolate cremas for me. Afterwards we took a tour around the schoolyard; I had no idea what they were telling me, but I nodded anyways. Then they all cheerfully sent me out the St. Gabriel's School gate waving and saying in sweet harmonic unison, "Good-bye."

At dinner we talked of my adventures around Lascahobas. Pol told me that St. Gabriel's School was built by Pere Blot when he was pastor, and it is the only school in the parish. Pol was trying to start some schools, out in the countryside at some of the chapels.

"Get some rest." Pol said, "Because tonight is the big festival for the New Year. It starts at ten tonight."

I must have been tired, I did not hear the bells ring so Pol shook me awake at 10:00 and said, "Tom, wake up. They are starting."

I got ready quick as I could and went into the church, which was almost full. Sleepily I sat through two hours of singing and scripture readings in Kreyòl, but as we got closer to midnight, the church filled to capacity and started getting lively. At midnight the lights came on, the steeple bells rang; the people all broke out in joyous song to strong conga beats. Out came Pè Pol and Pè Jethro in white vestments, wreathed in the smoky incense that they were carrying. It was very dramatic and impressive.

Mass proceeded, and at one point they brought out a large charcoal fire and placed it up in front of the middle aisle. "The fire code wouldn't allow this in the States." I thought. Then people were instructed to bring up pieces of paper, upon which were written their sins, and they placed them into the charcoal, which ignited them into flames. Afterwards, they went up to hand washing stations to finally clean their sins away.

Finally we came to the part where Pè Pol told everyone, "Bon Ane!" They all responded as the choir and drums started picking up the tempo, and the whole congregation exploded in song, and hugs, and jumping. Everybody getting up and wishing each other a Bon Ane: Happy New Year. It went on for 15 minutes, and I think Pol was working the crowd, shaking hands with every person in the church: every single one.

"I think I'm awake now." I remember thinking. We finished about 2am and when we returned to the rectory, the table was set. "What's this?" I asked.

"It's New Year's." Pol explained. "We have to eat our Soup Joumou." On the table was a glass bowl of a thick yellowish orange soup, with meat and vegetables. Joumou is a type of squash/pumpkin that was brought to Haiti from Africa by the slaves, it roughly translates to pumpkin, but the flavor is more like butternut squash.

Remember that January 1, besides being New Year's Day, is Haitian Independence Day. While enslaved, Haitians grew joumou, but the French never allowed the Haitians to eat it: just for spite. On January 1st 1804, when they won their independence, Haitians took the joumou, made soup, and proclaimed, "Now we are free, we will eat the soup joumou." Ever since on New Year's Day, every Haitian has soup joumou for good luck, and in remembrance of their history. It is very delicious soup too.

After soup joumou, we said good-night, and quickly slept.

The morning came with another Mass for the children, followed by a blessing of the children out on the lawn. Afterwards, Pè Pol and Pè Jethro threw candy out to them. The rest of the day was spent talking and meeting with folks who were just enjoying the day away from the worries of life. It was a day for hope; Haiti really needs hope. Still as I went around and witnessed life in Lascahobas, life that seemed to be lived truly in community, I thought, "Maybe we are the ones who need hope."

It was another great day, a day of peace and rest and happiness for the Haitian people. In just one week of wandering, I had learned more about Haitians as a people than I did all the times I was working hard seeing them in those clinics. It has truly been eye opening. Poverty? Yes. Many needs? Absolutely, but what they lack in things, they more than make up in what they give each other. I was hooked on the Haitian people during that trip.

Pè Pol, motorcycle, and friends on the canoe crossing Lake Peligre.

7
In the Loop

Si travay bon bagay, moun nan rich la ta pran-l lontan.

If work were a good thing, the rich would have taken it a long time ago.

The next morning at breakfast, I realized that Pol and I had never talked about how I would get back to Port-au-Prince and catch my return flight. Thimothè had left days ago with Sheryl's group to visit Hinche. I told Pol the time my flight was to leave and he suggested, "Well. Pè Jethro and I will need the jeep to go to Hinche that day, so I guess you can take the bus back to Port-au-Prince."

Now I am adventurous, but not that adventurous. There wasn't much that I passed on the trip up here that looked like a Greyhound. My mind went immediately to those men holding onto the top of the banana truck, and I sure did not know my way around Port-au-Prince especially without Kreyòl.

"Uh, Pol." I said sheepishly. "I'm not sure I'd like that idea."

Pol continued eating, thought a bit, and then he slowly baritoned, "Ahhhh, I will make a plan!"

More silence. Then after a while, I somewhat reluctantly asked him what his plan was. He told me that we would get up at 3am and he would drive me to Port-au-Prince early so that he could return to pick up Pè Jethro and go to Hinche. It was early but I was liking it better than that bus thing. It really was a lot of work for him, and I really appreciated the effort.

We awoke in the darkness, and I was ready to start heading back home. I was amazed at how many people were out walking on the roads that early in the morning. Pol told me, "They like to walk and do their work before the sun gets hot."

We arrived at the Port-au-Prince airport easily without much traffic, but too early for the airport to be opened yet. Pol dropped me off, we said our good-byes, and I just sat there alone for two-and-a-half hours until the airport opened. I had time to reflect on my first twinning trip to Haiti, and I recalled how random and wandering of a trip it had been. Still, I was helped by so many strangers, and I met some interesting people. I really had a better feel for Haiti. Pè Pol seemed genuine and I liked his buoyancy and love of people. We should work well together. Pol suggested that education was the number one desire of the people. I found that interesting given all of their other needs, but it made sense, and it reflected well on their priorities: children first. I needed to improve my Kreyòl skills in order to get to know, and to better understand my Haitian friends.

Weeks later while back home, I started talking to people about the trip, and several questions came up. People were amazed that I would even go to Haiti. "Isn't it dangerous down there?" They would say.

And many were surprised that my wife Leah would even "let me go." Her reply was something like, "What else was I going to do. Tie him down?"

I have often thought about that question, "Why Haiti?" and although I am moved by the poverty and the deteriorating infrastructure there, I am not really overly bothered by it. I can see the strength of the people shining above and through, and overshadowing those physical shortfalls. I think my experiences growing up have a lot to do with that.

I am the second oldest in a family of nine children. I had typhoid fever when I was three years old, and even at that age I vividly remember my entire hospital experience. It may have been one of the reasons I wanted to become a pediatrician. Our parent's marriage was a mixture of first generation immigrant families. My mother's side escaped Germany before Hitler, and my Dad's father was only five years old when he came over from Sicily on a boat by himself.

My grandfather, Santo Fama, lost both of his parents before leaving Sicily; he was sent to be raised by his cousins in Rochester, New York. Santo learned tile and stonework and married a nice Italian lady named Stella. They had two children, my dad Samuel, and then my aunt. Unfortunately when my dad was three, the family was in a car accident and I was always told that my grandfather Santo had died then. My dad worked in a butcher shop plucking feathers at five years old to help the family through the depression. My grandmother Stella worked as a seamstress. When I was about five, my dad went to a funeral, and I found out it was for my grandfather Santo who had been in an institution all of these many years with severe brain injury.

My aunt married early, leaving my dad and his mom to take care of each other. Stella could not remarry because her husband was still alive in the institution. During W.W. II my dad sent home his paychecks, which Stella saved, never spending them. When my dad finally returned from Europe, they used this money to buy a house, and lived there together until my father married. I remember my early years being happy, even though my German grandmother lived with us while she was dying of breast cancer. Grandma Josephine was a wonderful woman, always kind and faith filled even in her suffering.

My dad took on several jobs; he was a natural salesman. He had an insurance office in downtown Rochester, when in the mid 1960's the corner bar came up for sale, and he bought it as an investment. Over time it became clear that he would have to spend more and more time managing this pool and beer joint. He always took us to his office on Saturdays, to give my mom a break, and so afterwards we just started going to the bar, "The Loop Lounge," as well. It was right on the city's Inner Loop expressway.

The 'Loop,' as we called it was a poor white, country music playing sort of place when my dad took it over. Dad would put us to work sweeping, cleaning beer and cigarette smoke off of everything, bringing up beer, and any other jobs he needed done. We would then just sit around the bar the rest of the day waiting for dad's commands. It was boring, but we did get to meet some interesting people to say the least. If we were lucky, Dad would give us a roll of pennies and we would take them down to Hop Sing's Chinese restaurant to buy each of us an egg roll. Mr. Sing would always make us wait until he counted every single penny, and then yell at us in Chinese if he was short a penny. My two brothers and I would then have to go out and walk the streets until we found a penny on the curb. I often wondered how many times there were 51 cents and he let it go.

In the late 60's the clientele at the Loop changed, and it became a black bar, with a heavy Motown selection on the jukebox. We knew all sorts of characters, and became very comfortable with everyone there. There was Jake, a man who I really thought was nice and easygoing, but he got divorced twice. His wives kept coming in complaining about him, and I thought, "Wow, I like Jake, he's a good guy. I wonder what her problem is?"

My dad would say, "I'd be a nice guy too if I just sat around in a bar drinking beer and shooting pool all night."

We had Hubbie Lewis, this man could really talk some trash, I remember once he told us "He was so bad, that he had been to Attica Prison for life . . . twice."

The O'Donnahue twins, they were good Irish boys. They would drink all evening and then just take home some beers for the night: a whole case, which I am sure they drank as well.

My dad had some rooms in nearby houses that he rented out, mostly to the Loop customers. These stories could fill another book, but I clearly remember one guy who was stranger than the rest: very odd. Every evening he would leave the bar with one six-pack mumbling to himself. After six months of being behind on his rent, my dad had to finally ask him to leave. My dad had many people in those apartments who did not pay rent for months. He always let them stay until they could find another place to go. "I can't throw him out on the street." He would say. Anyhow, we were sent up to clean out his room, as was our usual job. The minute we opened the door of his room we smelled it: rotting beer. The room was covered with hoards of cockroaches, and the floor and the closet were filled with stacks of opened six-packs, filled with beer. It was the worst job my brothers and I ever had to do. We were physically sick dumping it all out amidst that army of cockroaches and the smell of stale beer. We had other jobs similar to that over the years. With those memories, Haiti did not always seem so bad.

As we got older, we would tend the bar. Actually we started bartending at age 16, my dad told us that there was a special law stating that you could tend bar at age 16 if your dad was the owner. I believed it, so one day when the police came in to question my age, I told the story so convincingly that he spent 30 minutes checking it out with his A.B.C. manual. Finally he told me he would have to 'take me in.' He threw me into the back of his cruiser and closed the bar. Right about then my dad showed up asking what was going on, and they let me go, but took dad downtown. It all worked out in the end with my dad telling a good story about me being a Boy Scout and all that. I think the jailor was one of his customers as well.

There was a lot of racial turmoil in the late 60's, but here at this mostly black bar with white owners, we did not have much trouble. Everyone was respected as long as they behaved, and I really was color-blind to it all. I remember a young black kid who poked his head in the door and asked, "Could I come in and buy some cigarettes for my dad?"

"Well of course you can." I told him surprised at his cautious question. I was later told that a lot of people were here from the south, and that they would never enter a place owned by white folks unless they asked permission first.

We would often order take-out from Hop Sing's. Once, a somewhat older black man named Clarence who was a regular customer and a good friend ordered a large take-out. When the food came I remember him saying, "This food stink-good!" When we shared the meal, and ate it together out of the same box he started chuckling. I asked him what was so funny and he said, "I never thought I'd live to see the day when a white man and a black man would eat out of the same bowl."

I always remember how odd that comment struck me, it was a shock to him, but I really had not even thought about it. Being comfortable with different people, and their problems were some of the lessons I learned at the Loop. I always thought that the reason I became a doctor, was from my experiences at the Loop; it's not much different than what I do now. People would come in and tell me their problems, and I would suggest a treatment, "Sounds like a rum and coke to me."

Although my dad was running a business, he showed concern and was always doing things for the street people who came around. If some of his rooms were empty, dad would let them stay there. He would let the homeless use the bar address to mail their government checks, and many of them he would put on weekly allowances so that they would not spend it all at once. He used to have us run to the store to get groceries for the elderly people who lived in the neighborhood, and he would give food and clothes out sometimes as well. What a double life for my brothers and me, weekdays at the Catholic school, and weekends at the Loop. Maybe it was not so odd after all.

I always wanted to be a doctor to help children, and was surprised to learn later in life that I could do fairly well in school. I had always thought that I was below average because it was hard for me to read. I got through college and went to Houston, Texas to medical school. I was excited by the warm weather, and about how different Texas was from New York.

I developed a good friendship with one of my classmates named Eric Barnhart; we have remained friends ever since. He and I would camp and later took two adventures into Mexico. During one of our two-week spring breaks, we drove to far southwest Texas, and crossed into Mexico at a small border bridge at Presidio. It was very remote and foreign; I loved the adventure of it all. We drove all the way to Mazatlan on the pacific coast of south Mexico guided only by my high school Spanish. I remember crossing the 'Tropico de Cancer' and could not believe we had driven that far. We got lost in the Mexican Rockies, and almost drove off the mountain after traveling all night. We wandered the Mexican side of Mazatlan, preferring our $5.00 a night local hotel to the glitzy tourist high-rises down the beach. We met local shrimp canners. They let us try some of the dried shrimp heads they would get from work, and eat as a snack. After trying some, I understand why the cannery threw them away.

On the way back over the mountains, our car broke down and we walked up to meet some local farmers to ask for help.

After our car was fixed, we went on our way, and later saw a ten-year-old sitting in a truck abandoned on the side of the road. He was waiting for his dad to bring gas for the truck, so we gave him some bread and made sure he would be ok. Later when our own car overheated on the side of the road, we saw the same ten-year-old driving the pick-up truck, honking as he passed us. The ten year old was driving; he never stopped for us.

Years later Eric and I took a similar trip riding buses and trains through Mexico's 'Barranca Del Cobre' or Copper Canyon, definitely not on the Triple-A tour either. We crossed the border at El Paso, Texas walking to the bus station in Juárez, Mexico. From Juárez we traveled to Chihuahua where we caught the Rail Mexico train that ran along the canyon rim. It was an exciting ride, with beautiful views of the canyon, the tropical forests, and the wildlife. We saw flocks of parakeets flying from the treetops. At our midway point, we stopped at a little way station town called Divisadero.

From this spot on the canyon's rim, we could see views down three of the great canyons: Del Cobre, Urique, and Tararecua. We spent a few nights there, and had been told of a hike to some natural warm springs down at the base of one of the canyons, so we decided to visit. We were told that we might run into the native peoples who inhabit the canyon, they are the Tarahumara people. They are the most prehistoric group of peoples in the Western Hemisphere, and are descended from the Anasazi or 'Ancient Ones.' They live a stone age existence in family groups within caves or temporary structures built into the sides of the canyon walls. They still speak an ancient language called Uto-Aztecan. One of their biggest social events is a ceremonial long distance run, which can last as long as three days.

We reached the hot spring, and although we could see some of the Tarahumara cave structures along the canyon walls, we did not see any Tarahumara themselves. While soaking in the natural hot springs, we finally saw them hiding behind rocks watching us. The Tarahumara are known to be very shy, but with time an older woman came and sat by the trail selling some handmade Indian dolls. She had an old cardboard sign with the prices written using charred wood. The woman appeared old and weathered, she was small and thin, with wrinkled skin, and never looked us in the eye. We bought a doll from her and walked back to town.

There were many other stories from these trips that I will not go into. All of these experiences taught me to be comfortable while visiting different places or with meeting people from different cultures, especially those who were materially poor. I might be naive, but I tend to trust people, and so far I have gotten away with this. A Haitian man once cautioned me about how I travel in Haiti, "Chak jou pa Dimanch." (Every day isn't Sunday) he told me. Maybe I have been lucky, or maybe it's true that God looks over fools and little children; I am too old to be a child, so that only leaves one choice. I tend to think I have learned to trust in the goodness of people, and when I approach others in that way, they respond in kind by trusting me. It's like when I faced those vicious dogs in Jamaica, I just stood there not retreating and not advancing, so they just passed me by: peacefully.

Question

8
The Question

Grangou se mizè, vant plen se traka.

Hunger is misery; a stomach that is too full is trouble too.

Life in Salem Virginia was back to normal; I was with my family and working at the clinic. Several people had shown an interest in the trip to Haiti and my experiences. Many of them wanted to visit Haiti, and I was itching to get back there myself. Pè Pol and I had corresponded by mail, and curiosity began to grow within the parish.

A group of four people got together for a trip in May of 1998; they all received their shots and passports, and off we went. The traveling went well, and it was nice having company this time. Thimothè picked us up at the airport; and we stayed at Visitation House with Ron.

While the group was getting settled in, I had a talk with Thimothè out on the lawn. I liked this quiet area out in back of Visitation House proper. As we sat, I noticed that the sun was going down. The lawn was surrounded by flowering plants, and shade trees. I could hear the boys over the wall on the Park Izmery field playing soccer. I wanted to talk with Thimothè about Haiti and get his opinion on something. I had heard about other groups who came down to Haiti with work crews to build churches or schools for people. I wondered if this was something we should think about doing as well. After asking him this, Thimothè was fairly silent at first; I have found that Haitians would rather say nothing than tell you bad news.

"Come on Thimothè. I'd really like to know, is this a good approach or not?" I persisted.

Thimothè turned and looked right at me, seriously but not threateningly, "Tom. It's an ok thing, but many Haitians need work. And many Haitians know how to build schools and churches; they'd like a job building them. So although it is a good thing, it would be better if you could help the Haitian people get jobs to build these projects." Afterwards we just sat there together enjoying the evening, and the cool breeze.

What Thimothè said made a lot of sense to me. It has to be degrading having someone do things for you all the time. It's not that Haitians are lazy or dumb, they just lack resources. It's like Ron once told me, "Unemployment in Haiti is high, but everybody is working." And from what I have seen, they work hard. Charity needs to be done with respect for the person you are trying to help, or it defeats the purpose.

"Thimothè," I said, "thanks for the advice. I guess we'll see you in the morning for our trip to Lascahobas." I then left to go upstairs with the others.

The group enjoyed the morning trip up Mon Kabrit on our way towards Lascahobas; we again made a stop in Mirebalais to buy straw hats. The road conditions had not changed along the way, it was just hotter. In Lascahobas Pè Pol welcomed us all, and we had a nice meal together along with Thimothè and Pè Jethro. At dinner everyone got along well with Pol, and he was just as animated and jovial as I had remembered. I practiced a few of my Kreyòl words from last visit, and that made Pol and Jethro laugh.

"Pol, are we going across the river again?" I asked.

"No Tom, but we are going to visit another outstation in a few days." Pol replied.

We toured the church and yard after dinner, and then went to our rooms. I showed them the shower and how to use the bucket method for bathing. I also warned them about the 5am wake-up bells; tomorrow would be the big Sunday Masses.

During Mass we split up and sat at different places so that we would not be all bunched together in one imposing group. Early during the service a dog walked into the front of the church and sat down, front and center, as if participating. "I guess all of God's creatures are welcome here," I thought. I had never seen that before, and I chuckled to myself. Finally the dog walked out the back.

Later during the offertory I saw Tifi walking into the front of the church; it was good to see her again, walking stick and all. She came in front and center, right at the most prayerful part of the Mass; I did not think that this was an accident either. She spotted us and slowly made her way along the aisle with her hand out to the congregants. Some gave her small coins; others just seemed to chastise her as if to say, "Why are you coming into Mass like this?"

She walked up to me and looked up with those eyes of hers; I just held her under my arm next to my side. She then started showing me with hand gestures how to pray during this part of the Mass, either with open palms or with her delicate bent fingers and hands together. I realized that she understood what was going on, and had more going on inside of her than met the eye. It was very prayerful and she seemed to want to help me, knowing that I was a stranger. With time she just got up and slowly shuffled out the back. I thought about that dog earlier, and I could not help but make the connection. Tifi was like this little stray dog; she is the human equivalent of the town's stray dog. I reflected on this the rest of the service.

That afternoon I wanted to take the group around town, so we started out in the square. I lined everyone up for a group photo in front of the church when suddenly I heard some commands being yelled at us. They were from a uniformed man coming out of the police compound, "No foto! No foto!" he was saying as he hurried towards us with fingers pointing and hands signaling "No!"

Although loud, he did not seem threatening, so I just told the group to continue setting up and told him that I was almost finished, just one more photo. He persisted yelling and at one point pulled out his old pistol and shook it at me. After I took my photos I figured it was time to play his game; I could see his uniformed comrades at the station laughing somewhat at his show of authority. Our man wore an older uniform than the other policemen, and I gathered he was a former Duvalier army thug accustomed to ordering folks around.

We let him lead us over to the station, his comrades still snickering as we entered the station. I tried to tell him, "Me friend, Pè Pol. Pè Pol friend." And I took out some photos of us together that I had in my pocket. Once he saw those I think he understood, but saving face he made gestures towards this book as if to say, "You need to sign in before you visit Lascahobas."

I do not know why but I argued with him saying, "We don't need to sign in with you guys! We're just visiting here." But letting it go, we signed his book, and I guess after that we were officially visitors in town.

We went around town giving photos to people I had seen on my last visit, and Jean Claude was certainly on that list. So we headed down the alleyway to his house and workshop. Coming into the open area I could not see anyone but said "Hello." I heard a response but I could not figure out where the sound was coming from. Suddenly out from the dump truck's bed arose Jean Claude smiling, followed by his family and wife. They had been sitting in the truck's bed having a quiet lunch together. The family climbed down from the truck bed and gave us hugs; they seemed very excited and surprised that we had returned. We made our introductions and then were offered seats.

We sat and talked and showed them the pictures we had taken, they were happy with the gift of family photos. It was nice reconnecting with Jean Claude and the family; the baby had grown, and everyone looked happy and healthy. Mom was proudly bouncing her now one-year-old naked son on her knee. We took some new photos for them, and I noticed that their dump truck was missing its tires and wheels and was now resting on the ground. I pointed this out to Jean Claude and he just laughed and said something unrecognizable. We all said good-bye with promises of return in the future.

We walked around the rest of town and saw men playing dominoes, and families at home with their children playing or just talking. People were always happy for us to visit and sit and spend a few minutes communicating in whatever way we could. But you could really see on a Sunday how much time families spend together with each other. It was just a slow and peaceful day before tomorrow's trip in the country to visit the Sacre Coeur Chapel in Cabestor.

The next morning after breakfast we left for Cabestor. We were told that we would have to walk some, and Pol took along some boys to carry water and a little food. We started out in the Land Rover which Justin, the young man on our trip, found very cool. After leaving town, we crossed the Lascahobas River, crunching over river rocks and splashing through the low water while the morning sun shimmered off the river's surface. Women were seen washing clothes by the river again, with a patchwork of colored clothes drying on the rocks behind them.

Out on the country road, it was very rugged and rough, but we 4-wheeled over it with just enough shaking and jarring to make it exciting. "I've got to get myself one of these!" Justin could be heard saying. We finally stopped at the end of the road, but the beginning of the trail.

"This is where we walk." Pol told us, as he parked the car in the brush on the side of the road.

We were at the trailhead, which began as the road ended, I could see the lush green valley laid out before us with rolling hills, and bordered by two high ridges. It was good to walk, I felt very connected to the people who were walking along with us, although they moved much faster and with greater skill than we did. We were a curiosity, and they smiled and returned our "Bonjou." with the usual "M'pa pi mal." (I'm not so bad). I guess that is the best you can ask for in Haiti: I'm not so bad.

It was hot just walking on these up and down trails, with mud and rocks and sharp plants pricking you, and we were not even carrying any heavy loads. But if you took the time every once in a while to look at the green fields next to those comforting mountains, and watched as a man worked his garden with an ox and plow under palm and coconut trees, turning the black fertile earth underneath, you got a sense that the land was good here.

At about the halfway point, we stopped at a small trailside market situated next to a stream. There was a lean-to structure under two large shady trees. Women were sitting on small chairs low to the ground in front of rice, or small cooking pots of food over a charcoal fire. "Bonjou." We said and they returned the greeting. I saw a young woman on a horse and I tried saying in Kreyòl, "I like your horse." To which she laughed hard. "What did I say?" I asked Pol.

"You told her you liked her horse, but she's riding a milet, a mule." Pol said while also laughing.

Hey I am a city boy, what do I know? Meanwhile one of the women came up to Kathy smiling and held both of her hands saying, “Mwen renmen ou.”

Pol smiled and translated, “She is telling you that she loves you. She is very happy you are visiting her.” Kathy replied in kind and was quite surprised at this show of affection towards a stranger. We all waved good-bye and went on.

The trail started leveling out, and we passed a grouping of houses on the side of the trail, people waved to us and to Pè Pol who seemed to know them. I heard, and could see, little children running and playing in their yards. Older women were helping to fix and comb the girls' hair, while mothers playfully chased after their little ones. The sounds and sights were of happy families together.

“We're almost to Cabestor.” Pol said.

I could see the stone chapel appearing through the mango trees. Sacre Coeur Chapel was situated on a large flat grassy yard with some fields of corn at the edges. It seemed to be fairly well built out of stone, with a tin roof, one of Pere Blot's projects. It had a small stone rectory out back, and a small banana bark structure with a tin roof in the yard near two large mango trees.

As we passed the stone chapel we could hear some voices inside, “That's the school.” Pol told us. We headed for the rectory to rest and drink some water; it was fairly basic inside the rectory, like a hunting cabin.

“Can we go over and visit the school?” I asked. And after some water we left to tour the school. In the dark church we saw four teachers, each teacher was standing in front of two small blackboards, with two groupings of children in front of each teacher. "What is going on in here?" I asked.

"This is the school. Many children want to go to school, but we don't have classes or teachers for them, so each teacher teaches two classes. There are no schools out here." Pol explained.

We went through the school, and the teachers all stood proudly in front of their classes and instructed their students to greet us. "Bonjou mon Pè." They all chimed as we passed, obviously very intrigued by their white visitors. The little ones seemed very frightened of us. I remembered thinking how dark it was in there; I could hardly read the blackboard. The children sat on benches, they did not have desks. I did not see any textbooks, although some of the children had pencils and notebooks.

After a while Pol asked. "Would you like to see the little school? Come. I show you outside."

We left the stone chapel-turned-schoolhouse, and went into the area outside that was shaded by the two large mango trees. Past the trees was a small weathered banana-bark sided structure with a rusty tin roof, and I could hear a class going on inside. We walked into the usual, "Bonjou mon Pè." I saw that the school was packed with the cutest little students, all in uniforms. It was hot, dusty and dark, and all I could see at first were their wide white eyes gazing needingly up at me. Curious at the sight of this strange visitor, I acknowledged the teacher and motioned the students to sit. Smiling approvingly I left after Pol explained the situation to the teacher.

It was hot outside, but all I could think about was how hot and stuffy it was in that little oven of a hut with its dirt floors. "How were these kids able to pay attention in there?" I thought.

Pol tapped me and said, “Here comes the director.”

I turned and saw this slender somewhat weathered man about fifty coming towards me. He had a distinguished look about him, his posture and how he carried himself, slowly and assuredly walking towards me for a greeting. He had a long French styled mustache. As we approached he extended his hand to me standing straight up, and greeted me in French, “Bonjour, monsieur. Je m'appelle Sonrius Jean Baptiste. C'est un grand plaisir de faire votre connaissance. Bienvenue à Cabestor.” (good morning sir, my name is Sonrius Jean Baptiste and It’s a pleasure to meet you. Welcome to Cabestor.) After saying this and clasping my hand, he clicked his heals together while making a small sharp bow at his waist. It impressed me as a very formal French sort of greeting.

I was impressed, and just returned a smile and said something less smart such as, “Hi, good to see you too.” Somewhat clumsily.

Sonrius joined Pol and myself on a bench under the mango trees. I listened as they spoke about what sounded like business in rapid Kreyòl. On occasion Sonrius would look over at me and smile in a friendly way, but he appeared to be a man who took his responsibilities seriously. Although a man of the country, Sonrius obviously has had some education and a sense of professionalism about him.

Pol stopped for a second to tell me, “Sonrius was telling me of all the children out here he is trying to educate. So many families want their children to go to school.” Pol said this with his usual cheeky tight-lipped smile and chuckle.

I left them to talk. The others were out on the churchyard turned soccer field, where the children were playing during recess. The children reminded me of any other group of children on recess, playing, talking loud, and running around chasing each other or kicking a ball-like object. The girls were all surrounding our women and wanted to feel their hair, and were quickly trying to put it into braids. They were fascinated by it. Justin was kicking the ball back with the boys. "Words are not the only way to communicate," I thought.

We spent the afternoon in Cabestor until the midday heat had calmed down, and then we walked back along the valley trail to the parked Land Rover, where we drove back to Lascahobas.

I was impressed by what Pè Pol was doing out in the countryside where there is little or no opportunity for education. We talked as a group during dinner that night about the day's experience. Pol was happy that everyone had such a good time. "Tom. Could we talk later?" Pol asked, and we agreed to meet.

Around dusk Pol was sitting outside the rectory on the lower covered patio. It is a quiet place facing a small garden next to the outside wall. There was an old well from which I could hear frogs croaking. The night was warm but comfortable, and I could hear voices from out on the street beyond the wall. I joined Pol on the bench and we talked.

"Tom. What did you think of the school?" Pol asked.

I commented. "I was glad to see that you've been giving the kids a chance to go to school. The kids seemed happy."

"It's a good start." Pol continued, "I have a plan to provide education for the children in the rural area of Cabestor. I would like to build a school for them out at the chapel. Here are some plans I'd like to show you." Then he brought out some papers with a drawing of a five room schoolhouse, and some itemized figures relating to construction costs. He went over the paper and the costs, and he showed me the final estimation of $49,000 U.S.

I commented, "Wow, that's great. The kids will really be happy with a new school. The old one is too dark and hot, and the chapel is noisy."

"Yes, this is why I want to build a new school. Tom, I want you to build it for me." Pol said pleadingly, his eyes looking right into mine.

Silence followed while I tried to comprehend what Pol had just told me. Then, I just sat there a bit shocked by what he had asked. I really did not expect a request like this. I did not have $49,000 on me at the time.

"Pè Pol." I said somewhat high voiced. "I don't have the money to build this. I don't know if the parish does either. We're just getting started on a project to build ourselves a new church."

Hearing myself say these words sounded so hollow; we need to spruce up our church and here Pol is trying to educate his kids and we cannot help. The two needs did not seem to hold equal weight.

Pol's face turned sad when I told him this. I could tell he spent a lot of time on the plans and he was really hoping I would just jump on it right away so he could get started. We just sat there next to each other for a while; I felt very small. Pol finally spoke in a depressed voice, one that I had never heard from this upbeat man before. "Well Tom. I was hoping you could help me, but I understand that this is a big project."

I was starting to feel pale as if I was watching someone die before me, and I was not doing anything to help him. Pol was my friend. We had shared some great times, we had shared meals together, and we had shared our hopes and dreams together. "Pol. You are my friend, I don't know what I can do, but I will try to see if I can help. I will try for you." I said these words half trying to lift Pol's spirits, and half because I thought, "Let's see what happens."

"Thank you." Pol replied, still looking like a man who had received news about the death of a loved one. His head hung down, but he did manage to look over at me with a smile.

"It must be hard for you Pol." I asked supportively. "So many needs. So many people."

"Yes. Everyday people come to me, sometimes we can help." Pol confessed. "Sometimes we can just pray for them. Today Pè Jethro used the jeep to take a woman with Typhoid to Mirebalais. But the children, I hate it when I can not help the children."

We sat together for a while listening to the frogs, and to the street voices coming from the other side of the wall. I could feel his burden. I could sense his helplessness. I knew of his desires that evening as we sat together. Something happened to me that evening; somehow I took on this responsibility, together with him as we talked. That moment was the point from which I would never be able to turn back, and I have not turned back since.

Back at Visitation House, I sat down with Ron and we talked about my experience with Pè Pol and his school proposal. Ron chuckled, "It didn't take him long to hit you up with something." Ron told me that education really is one of the big needs in Haiti, and of course Haiti has many needs. Ron gave me some information about the history of Haiti's problems with education, and statistics on the state of education in the country today. This is what I learned.

Education in Haiti has been a problem since the country's independence in 1804, when although the constitution established free education for everyone, this mandate has never been realized. The situation was so dire that in 1860, the Vatican struck a deal with the Haitian government to provide education through French religious orders. They instituted a French style of education, and unfortunately catered to the elite in Haiti, and downgraded the rural Haitians as being backwards and unruleable. Even with the church's help, the children in rural areas were not being served. French was the language at school, but families grow up speaking Kreyòl; so the families could not help with homework. This was another hindrance to learning for these rural families with no history of schooling.

The Church has continued to be the main source of education, especially in the poor areas, and thankfully they have reformed their system to include Kreyòl in the first few years of school, and then introduce French later on. By 1981 the school enrollment in rural areas had doubled from what it was in 1970, mostly from foreign aid. Still, most children in Haiti did not have access to education; more than 65% of the country's population over ten years of age had not received any formal education at all. Of course the children in rural areas are being underserved to a much great degree.

Presently the adult literacy rate is about 50% overall, with the rate of primary school enrollment at 65%. Many children who start primary school do not finish; only about 30% of these enrollees will complete the sixth grade. Of course these numbers are always worse in the rural areas. About 90% of Haiti's primary schools are private, and do not receive any aid from the government. The demand for education is great; Haitians place a high value on education as a way to better their lives, and their country's condition. Even in their poverty, it is estimated that Haitian families spend 15% of their household incomes on education. I had no idea of the extent of this problem.

The next day we spent an afternoon feeding and holding the babies with the Sisters of Charity at Mother Teresa's Hospital for sick and dying children. Looking into the eyes of those thin, coughing babies, and trying to get them to eat is powerfully disturbing. I was moved but not disheartened, this is just the reality of Haiti made visible to us. As the Haitian Proverb says, "What the eye does not see, the heart cannot feel." I know that at least these children would not be alone; they would be shown some dignity through human touch and human kindness.

The nursery was filled with cribs of babies, and the Sisters have images and statues of Mary along the walls. Seeing Mary standing there, her hands open and out, spoke to me as if she was saying, "Hold my babies. Love my babies." With one of her babies in my arms I could only rock him and weep. This orphanage is just the reality of Haiti. No one person can change it all, but I can hold this one child. I thought of Pol's children in Cabestor. What can I do for them?

I thought of this as we headed home to Virginia. It always feels good to get back home. Sometimes I am not sure where my home is anymore. I had a lot on my mind; Pè Pol's request was still weighing heavily on me, but I tried to put it out of my mind and just think about getting home. Maybe it will take care of itself: maybe.

9
Runnin' Scared

Si Bondye ki vole ou, li pral peye fre pou ou.

If it is God who sends you, he'll pay your expenses.

While back in Salem with my family and work, I thought a lot about those school children in Cabestor. I thought about my experience holding and feeding those children in Mother Teresa's Hospital. I thought about my friend Pè Pol, and the commitment I had made to him: a commitment to try and help. It seemed innocent enough, "I'll do my best," but there was something different about this promise. This promise would not be easy to keep nor easy to release myself from. Nothing was physically holding me to it, no legal papers or statutes. Something deeper held me; it was a promise not written on paper, but inscribed on my heart. I didn't know this at first, but would only come to realize it with time.

I returned to Salem quite excited about the experience, about all of the people I had met and the places we had gone. Kathy, Justin, and the others in the group were likewise talkative about all that had happened, and people seemed genuinely interested as well. I thought that with all of this excitement, people would be enthusiastic about Pol's project of building a new school. Our parish had been working on updating our own campus with new classrooms, offices, and a new worship space.

I took Pol's paper with the school diagram, figures, and specifications, and I presented it to our Parish Council and our pastor Father Gregory. He had been very supportive of our trips and the Haiti project. I briefly sat down with him and went over it all, and I told him about the need for finding the $49,000 to help them build their school. It seemed like a lot of money to me, but something doable. When Father Gregory saw this he reacted as I first did, "This is a lot of money Tom, and we aren't a rich parish. We're having trouble finding the money to build the changes we want for our parish. We haven't got that kind of money. Pè Pol just has the wrong parish to help him with his school. We can't do it, it's impossible." Gregory said.

I was taken aback when I heard this. I have to admit I thought the same thing originally, but I expected some help or words of encouragement such as, "Well it would be tough, but we can certainly try." Instead I found myself up against another wall. Now, as the pastor, Father Gregory had many responsibilities, and his newest one was trying to get his own church rebuilt. I know he was not even sure if he could get that done, so the thought of building a school in Haiti must have been just too much for him. Still, I did not know where to turn; I could tell that I was not going to get help from anyone else.

I thought about this for a few weeks. Whenever it was quiet, or I was driving home, or during that time just before sleep and wakefulness, I would think about how in the world I was going to help Pè Pol build his school? Finally one night, while changing my clothes to get ready for bed, I once again was alone and agonizing over this promise I had made. I was realizing that I just could not do it, it was impossible, yet I could not go back to Haiti and tell Pol I had not helped him. These were two irreconcilable realities that I had no solution for. The happy trap had been set, and I was caught: ensnared by love. I was physically feeling sick, nauseated, and in a sweat. I asked God to help me, "God I cannot do this, but it needs to be done. Please help me! I know you can help me." And I wept in my helplessness.

But then, and I don't know why, suddenly I just knew that everything was going to be ok. I just knew that somehow it would be done. All was right, and I went to bed peacefully for the first time since coming back from Haiti. After dreaming, I awoke the next morning and realized that in order to get this done, I needed to become a fundraiser. No one else was going to do this for me; it was up to me to find a way.

I invited Father Gregory to dinner at his favorite Chinese restaurant and we shared a meal. I told him more about my experiences with Jean Claude, and with Tifi. I told him about our walk to Cabestor and all the children packed into their makeshift school. He listened intently. Then I asked him once again for help, which again he could not promise.

So I asked him another simple question, "Can I at least ask people if they would help. Just give me permission to ask people."

He looked somewhat surprised by this, but after thinking about it he said, "Sure Tom, you certainly can try asking for help." He said this as if he had nothing to lose, it was not any extra responsibility for him, and he sounded certain that it would not go anywhere. He had been asking for money to renovate the church without much luck, so go ahead Tom and ask.

That was all I needed. I was on a mission; I needed to become a fundraiser, but how? Who should I go to and learn how to do this? I immediately thought of Estelle Nichols from the Bradley Free Clinic where I was volunteering. She had since married and was now Estelle Avner, and she is the most upbeat woman I know. I had watched her in action fundraising to keep the Free Clinic operating, and she is the best. When she asked you for help, you actually wanted to give her money. I always said that when Estelle walked by; you better check your wallet because she would probably have some of it for her

Clinic. So I approached her one evening after I finished my shift at the Free Clinic.

"Estelle?" I said, "I need to ask you some questions about fundraising. I have this project idea for Haiti." Now Estelle knew that I had gone to Haiti, but didn't know the specifics.

"Sure Tom, I would love to hear about it." Estelle replied with her enthusiastic smile. Estelle was genuine, that was what made her so good at making the Free Clinic successful. She always had time to sit and talk with people; she loved people and took the time to get to know them. "Come into my office and we'll talk."

We sat together for the evening and I told her my story, and she was quite fascinated. I asked her for help, and she was flattered that I respected her opinion about fundraising. Still, I think deep down she knew also that she was the best at this and Estelle was happy to share her secrets. "Tom, there's no problem with raising money; you just have to have a good story. And you have a good story. Now you have to find the right people to tell it to."

We talked some more, and she was very encouraging. I asked Estelle about foundations or grants, and she thought that these could be a possibility. Suddenly she had an idea. She and I were members of Rotary International, she knew of a man by the name of Reid Jones who had done some work in Haiti through Rotary years ago. He was a very giving man, who worked hard and had recently died leaving behind a large charitable foundation.

She looked through her desk drawer and papers until finally Estelle pulled out a scrap of paper with a scribbled name on it, "Ha haaaa!" She said, "Here it is. Reid Jones' charity is called the JOCO Foundation. I have the phone number for his daughter and for the lawyer who was handling the Foundation. They might be interested because Reid was very active in Haiti after he took a trip there with Rotary years ago." Estelle was very encouraging, and I left energized after obtaining this information and a lead on a possible grant.

This was a good start; but Estelle, although high on encouragement, was a little short on details. Who else did I know? John Pendarvis. John is the C.E.O. of Family Services of Roanoke, and had successfully run this charitable organization for years. I believe he was getting ready to expand into a new building as well. So John and I sat and talked. John is a very capable, careful, and professional man who seemed to care very much about his organization and its mission. He is a people person who leads with wisdom and heart. His advice was invaluable. He had organized a plan for me in a short time. He told me what was needed, and how I should go about it. All of this was very fresh on his mind, because of his fundraising efforts.

"Put a dinner together where you can tell people your story." I remember John saying. "You just have to start asking people. Also, you should have some money in hand by the time you get to that dinner."

I would try. I put together some photos of the trip, and some documents, and the drawings of the proposed school. Then I called some people to meet in their homes to tell my story. It reminded me of the time I sold magazines for the Boy Scouts, just about as difficult. I did get some folks who committed, and it was encouraging. But I needed to do more, I thought about this JOCO Foundation that Estelle had told me about.

I called Mr. Reid Jones' daughter Margaret, and she told me that the estate was still unresolved and in the hands of her father's lawyer. So I called Ms. Dianne E. Wilcox, Mr. Jones' lawyer, and I asked her about the foundation. She seemed very encouraging, and stated that the foundation was presently trying to build some schools in the Dominican Republic, which shares the island of Hispaniola with Haiti. She knew of Reid Jones' involvement and love of Haiti while he was in the Rotary Club of Roanoke. Over the phone I asked her if I could have a grant for $25,000 to get me started with my fundraising efforts. She thought that this amount was not unreasonable, and that she would have me meet with one of her associates and fellow board member, Jimmy Killinger. I took his phone number, but she assured me that he would call me.

I really had no idea what I was stepping into with this JOCO Foundation. It was months later that I found out its history. Reid Jones was a man who started out life without much, but worked very hard and was known to be somewhat miserly. Starting life as a salesman, he could talk his way through anything. After his business had grown, Dianne Wilcox was assigned from her law firm to assist Jones in selling his safety supplies to W.W. Grainger Company. The success of these sales made Reid Jones a multimillionaire. Even in his financial success, he was known to save paper clips and unused stamps, but with age he became more philanthropic. He gave money away generously to several local charitable organizations. His death was somewhat mysterious, even though he was very sick with emphysema and required oxygen.

Mr. Jones left behind an estate valued at over $12 million dollars, this would fund the JOCO Foundation. He had one daughter, Margaret Irvin, who he and his estranged wife adopted as an infant. The relationship between Margaret and her dad was very strained, but he did pay for her to get a first class education and it was thought that one day Margaret would take over her father's business. Days before his death, the estate was transferred from Margaret's control, to the control of Jones' lawyer: Dianne Wilcox. Although the will was being contested, I knew nothing of the behind-the-scenes problems when I finally contacted Jimmy Killinger asking for a grant from the JOCO Foundation.

Jimmy seemed friendly enough when I called, and he was eager to meet with me. His voice sounded country, like a western singer, not the same as Dianne's professional speech. He also told me about the school building projects that the JOCO Foundation was undertaking in the Dominican Republic. We agreed to meet at a Subway sandwich shop in Roanoke and talk some more. I put together a proposal letter, some of my Haiti photos, and the sketch of the school Pè Pol had given me. Looking back, I had no idea what I was doing, and although I tried to act professional I must have appeared pretty rinky-dink.

I arrived at the designated Subway shop slightly ahead of our scheduled appointment, somewhat anxious about what I was to say to convince the JOCO Foundation to give me this $25,000 grant. It did not occur to me that meeting a large foundation at a Subway store was somewhat unconventional. Still there I was, and I waited for over an hour: no Jimmy. Later, I called him and he apologized for coming at the wrong time, and said he had missed me. So we rescheduled, same Subway store.

I arrived early again. I sat with a drink as not to alarm the help, and I waited for another hour, only leaving long enough for a trip to the rest room. Later, when I called Jimmy he said he was running a little late, but that he was there. He walked in, and did not see me, so he left. "Did you go to the restroom?" he asked. "Maybe we missed each other. I'm sorry."

About that time I was feeling a little miffed, but he had this money I needed, so we agreed once more to a Subway rendezvous. He assured me he would come, and not leave this time.

I arrived a third time. I sat outside, no drinks this time, and I waited. Finally after 30 minutes a large new pickup truck with a shinny chrome toolbox on the back showed up. I noticed that hand painted on the side of the truck were the words 'Runnin' Scared.' I could tell that the driver was looking for someone and I called out to him, "Jimmy?" We shook hands and he apologized profusely for missing me the last two times.

Jimmy was a man about fifty years old, who looked and talked country, and appeared as if he had worked construction. Maybe it was the truck and toolbox. "Why does your truck say 'Runnin' Scared' on it?" I asked.

"Oh, that's just an inside joke." He said with a snicker. I showed him the papers and the proposal. He liked what he saw, and he felt comfortable working with me since I was not working for a big organization. "We like helping people who aren't connected to big groups." He told me. After he asked some questions he just said, "Sure, we can promise you $25,000 for your school as a matching grant if you can raise the rest. It's a done deal bud." And with that we shook hands and he rode off in 'Runnin' Scared.'

I was so excited to have this pledge, that I never thought about the fact that no papers where signed; only a handshake and some phone numbers were exchanged. I saw John Pendarvis soon after that and I told him the news; I was elated, but I remember him looking perplexed about the way that the whole thing unfolded. Still he was happy for me.

I put together a dinner at a local country club, invited Bishop Sullivan as our honored guest, and made arrangements to fly Pè Pol to Roanoke to speak along with me at the dinner. Invitations were sent, and I had a friend, Jeff Krajnik, who just finished architecture school draw a large sketch of the school. "I want people to see what it is we're trying to build in Haiti." I remember saying. All was set; I had my seed money, my grant, and a room full of people to 'tell my story to' as Estelle had instructed.

Waiting at the airport for Pè Pol to arrive, I was not sure whether he would show up or not. He had received the tickets that I sent down with Sheryl and her group a few months ago, but I had not heard from him since. So I was happy to see Pol walk across the tarmac with his bag. He was wearing a beret and a large smile when coming into the terminal. We were both happy to see each other and I was glad that he made the trip ok.

Driving to my home, I had to wonder what he thought of the U.S. coming from Haiti. He had visited the U.S. before, so it was not new to him. Pol had only brought a small carry-on bag with him; I remember being impressed by the simplicity of his needs. After he was situated in his room, I took him outside where my kids had a trampoline. "What's that?" he asked.

I showed him how the trampoline worked, and he just started laughing with excitement as he took off his shoes and wanted to try it. He got up on it and started jumping, only to fall all over the place in childlike laughter. We sat together on that trampoline for a few minutes looking at the trees and sky, and instantly rekindled our friendship. He is such a personable gentleman; I knew that people would connect with him well at our dinner.

"Tom." Pol said "I'm glad to visit with you my friend, but I have news for you. The new Bishop is moving me to another parish in a few months."

Now this was a shock to me, we had this friendship, and I did not want the people at the dinner to be confused as to who as pastor they were supporting. "Pol." I said, "Let's not say anything about this just yet. For now, you are our man in Haiti. We'll have to deal with a new priest later."

I was saddened by this news, but our work is with the community, not with an individual. I knew that one day he would be moved; his new parish was just down the road from Lascahobas in Belladaire so we would be able to visit. I had too much going on to worry about this now.

One day Pol and I took a trip to Wal-Mart and he was just in awe by the size of the place, and the amount of stuff for sale. "We don't have one store this big in all of Haiti." He said. We did some shopping, and later Pol asked me about our money. "It says on here, 'In God we Trust.' Does that mean that money is God in America?"

Good question really, "No Pol, but it's a good observation." I replied. But with the size of Wal-Mart, maybe it is in the Dollar we trust.

We drove around and visited several of the folks from our previous trips, and he commented on how each car had only one person in it where in Haiti one tap-tap is packed with people. He was surprised to see very few people walking, and that all the roads were paved. "You don't have any mud here." He commented.

With Pol visiting, I could see the contrast between life in Haiti, materially poor, but rich in community. And life in the U.S., materially rich, but somehow separated from community. We all ride in separate cars and live separated in our homes. There is not the mix of life on the street and in the rectory yard that we saw in Haiti. Pol got some rest as we waited for the big fundraising dinner.

Everything was set. The room was in order with table decorations reflecting Haitian proverbs. The food was ready, and Jeff Krajnik had placed the large drawing of the proposed school out front. The turnout was good, and everyone enjoyed meeting Pè Pol, as I knew they would. Then we told our story, with a slide show of some of the people in Lascahobas and Cabestor, and we showed what life was like in Haiti. We showed the children, and told about the need for education in the countryside. I also told people about how providing money for the construction of the school would provide dignity and a sense of local ownership to the project; how this school would be a symbol of hope for the people. It would also infuse needed money into this poor community, which would then circulate many times over. People were moved, and impressed by the fact that we already had $35,000 in seed money including our grant. By the time the evening was over, we did not get the $49,000 we needed. Instead we had over $70,000!

"Pol." I said, "I think we're gonna' build you an eight room schoolhouse instead of the five you asked for. Do you think you can fill it with kids?"

With Pol's usual deep throaty chuckle he responded, "Yes Tom, I think they are already filled." It was a great feeling, and we just sat and talked that night about his dreams for Haiti, and how he knew that we would get the school built. His only regret was that he would be leaving the parish.

"Who is the new priest in Lascahobas?" I asked.

"His name is Pè Hermann Heriveaux. He's a friend of mine, and is now the pastor in Mirebalais." Pol replied.

"Oh." I thought to myself. "I know this man." When we would pass through Mirebalais and stop at his parish, he would usually go up to his room and not interact with the Americans who visited. I had heard from Adele that he did not want to bother with a twinning relationship, and he did not know why he would have to fill out a form telling someone in the U.S. about his parish. "It's none of their business." I think is what Adele told me he said. I had never met him, but he sounded less agreeable than Pol. This was going to be a problem, now that I had this money; I needed to trust the person receiving it, and make sure they were going to use it as intended. There have been reports of priests stealing the money, or using it for other projects of their choosing, and not for the original purpose. This could be a big problem; I'll have to deal with it later.

Two days after the dinner things seemed to settle down until I picked up the newspaper, and on the front page was an article about the JOCO Foundation. The lawyer, Dianne Wilcox and her associates where all being investigated for inappropriate handling of Mr. Reid's estate. "Oh, no!" I thought, "This is not good." I need to ask for that money before the estate is frozen. Pol had left to go back to Haiti that morning, and I started calling Jimmy and Dianne. There either was no answer, or I was reassured by Jimmy that "He would take care of it." He never did.

This went on for a few months, until finally Dianne answered the phone and finally mailed me the check from the JOCO Foundation. Meanwhile the story was unfolding in the newspaper about the whole affair. Mr. Reid's lawyer, Dianne Wilcox, had the will changed and witnessed just three days before his death, a death that was suspicious for suffocation on top of his emphysema. Out of the $12 million estate, 'the board' had spent all but $1 million; much of it in the Dominican Republic, building some schools but also a large home. The contractor in the Dominican Republic was still owed money, and eventually bulldozed the schools to the ground. Dianne Wilcox was disbarred, and I never heard from Jimmy Killinger again, but something tells me he was runnin' scared.

I cashed that JOCO Foundation check as soon as I received it, and I was happy to have it clear. We started collecting the money for the school; and my next task was to find out who Pè Hermann was, and how we were going to work with him.

I arranged a dinner meeting with Father Gregory to update him on the progress of the fundraising; we met again at his favorite Chinese restaurant. Father Gregory was absolutely stunned, “I can’t believe it!” He said.

I reminded him that it was at this same restaurant that he said it would be impossible. I also reminded him that with God all things are possible.

Lascahobas River, route from Village to Cabestor.

Water girl, walking through the Cabestor Valley.

10
Pè Hermann

Tout moun se moun, men tout moun pa menm.

All people are people, but all people are not the same.

Just when I reached one summit, there seemed to be another mountain to climb. I could relate to the Haitian proverb, Deyen mon gen mon: beyond this mountain is another mountain. Now that the money was pledged for the school construction, I had to make sure that a school is indeed what would be built. I was responsible for how this money was spent in Haiti, and I would be putting the money into the hands of an unknown priest, whom I have heard is not that excited about working with outsiders. How was I to get the money to Haiti? I did not see many banks in Lascahobas. We would just have to start from the beginning as we did with Pè Pol, and go down to Haiti to build a new relationship with this man: Pè Hermann.

I was lucky on this trip to be accompanied by Jean Denton, although this was her first parish trip with me, she had visited Haiti about twenty years ago as a member of a group from the press coming to write about Haiti. Jean is a part time writer, and a full time illustrator, who has the gift of listening and patience. She has a wonderful 'woman's intuition' about people that I would find invaluable for the task of connecting to Pè Hermann. I had collected enough money to get started on the school construction. I really did not know how else to get it there other than to just carry the money with me, so I brought a check for $35,000 with me to Haiti. I felt fairly vulnerable carrying this much money, and going into Haiti. I really did not want to advertise this, especially to Hermann until we could feel him out.

I did not declare the money coming into customs telling myself, "Well I really don't have any money, just a check." I felt like I was sneaking it into the country, sort of like a drug dealer or something. When we got to Visitation House and were all settled in, I told Ron about my dilemma and he suggested, "Why don't you just use Fonkoze? It's a new bank for the poor that was started a few years ago, in fact they're having a meeting here tonight. You can meet the founders." That sounded great to me.

After our evening meal, people started arriving for the Fonkoze meeting. A Haitian priest came in by the name of Pè Joseph Philippe. With him was a wiry American woman named Anne Hastings. She had a short efficient haircut, to match her energetic organized demeanor. We were introduced, and later I was able to speak with both of them about their organization.

Fonkoze was the idea of Pè Philippe; the name stands for Fondasyon Kole Zepòl (Foundation shoulder-to-shoulder). Pè Philippe noticed that people were able to get political control of their country after voting for President Aristide, but that they also needed to become economically freed from those powers that kept them trapped in poverty. Access to capital, and the knowledge of how to begin and sustain a small business was all that was lacking. He also noticed that women were the economic force that could propel his grassroots effort towards 'economic democracy' forward. Banks were not serving the poor fairly, and Pè Philippe realized that he needed to create a totally new bank for the poor from the ground up, a bank that they could call their own, and that would serve their needs fairly.

In 1995 Pè Philippe, along with some grassroots leaders, founded Fonkoze to do just that. But he was a priest, and knew nothing about starting a bank. Enter Anne Hastings who was a very successful Washington, D.C. management consultant who was looking to do more with her life; she had just joined the Peace Corps. Although originally assigned to Africa, after her resume was read, she was asked if she had any interest in Haiti. They knew of a priest there that was doing amazing work, and could use her skills.

A few days later she had a phone message that simply said, "This is Father Joseph Philippe, we are very pleased you have decided to work with us in Haiti. You may be the director of our new bank: Fonkoze. Thank you." Anne met with Father Philippe and immediately came to the realization that he had more vision than all of the top executives she had worked with in her D.C. consulting firm. Father Philippe sat down with her, pulled up his old typewriter on this rickety old table, and they got to work creating Fonkoze. She agreed to 'give it a try' for nine months, and she has never looked back since.

Fonkoze has become THE bank for the rural poor in Haiti, and has been recognized globally as a leader in micro credit. They not only lend money at reasonable rates, but also educate and foster businesses. Most importantly for our needs, they wire transfer money from the U.S. securely for a reasonable fee, then change the dollars into goudes at fair market rates. Anne even knew Pè Hermann, "He helped us open our bank in Mirebalais when he was pastor there." She told me.

This was great information; I am always amazed at what I can learn at Visitation House and from Ron Voss. Ron encouraged me to use their services, which in turn would help the Fonkoze organization grow. I asked Ron about how I could make sure the money I gave the parish was used in the way it was intended, it did not seem like legal agreements held much water in Haiti.

Ron suggested, "What you have to do Tom, is talk to the community. Everything is done within the context of community. If you make a public statement and tell everyone that you're sending this money, and it's supposed to go for a school in Cabestor, then they will all be watching Fr. Hermann. You have to make it public so that everyone knows what's going on."

That sounded like good advice as well, I will need to talk to the whole parish when I get to Lascahobas. Jean was also impressed by Ron, and all that Pè Philippe and Anne Hastings were doing for Haiti. Tomorrow we would be on our way to meet Pè Hermann.

Thimothè drove us up Mon Kabrit and to Lascahobas where we were greeted by Pè Hermann. He was friendly enough and graciously showed us around the churchyard. Hermann has a small build with a neatly cropped mustache, and although polite, he did not seem to have the gregarious nature and natural love of people that Pol had. Hermann had done some repairs to the rectory, and we had some running water to wash our hands before dinner.

We sat and talked during dinner, which consisted of fried goat, beans and rice, boiled bananas with sauce, and fresh avocados. It was all delicious. Hermann did not speak much English, but knew some words; his associate priest Pè Bertrand translated for us. We had some laughs and began to break the ice, but it was not as easy as with Pol.

I asked Hermann, "Did Pè Pol tell you about our school project?"

"Yes, I know of it." Hermann replied in Kreyòl. "Pè Pol is my friend, we all work together."

"Can we go down and visit Cabestor?" I asked.

"If you want to. But I don't think we can because of the rain. Mud is on the road." Hermann explained. Then silence, and he started talking with Pè Bertrand in Kreyòl.

I persisted, "You know, I would really like to visit the teachers and see the kids again. I'd be fine with just walking there myself."

"No Tom!" Hermann said somewhat sharply.

Pè Bertrand explained, "Pè Herman doesn't want you to go. He hasn't had a chance to meet with the people in Cabestor and establish himself as pastor. He'd like to do that before you go and visit again."

I was not really happy with this, but I guess he is the boss. I was really looking forward to visiting them again.

I realized how difficult it was to communicate without knowing Kreyòl. Pè Pol had always worked on his English and spoke rather well. Although Hermann knew some English, it was not enough for a more detailed talk. This makes it tough to form a bond. I also thought about the fact that I am a guest in Haiti, and to expect the Haitians to learn my language was a bit arrogant. If I am going to respect them, I need to come and learn their language while I am in their country. "I need to learn Kreyòl when I get back, and I will work on it here as well," I told myself.

The next morning we went to Mass, and Hermann seemed formal with the people. Still he was respected, but I did not notice the affection people had for Pol. I told myself that this is probably typical for a new priest. Hermann was going to Mirebalais for the day, and asked us along. We arrived at St. Louis' Church rectory, his old parish, for a meeting of several priests. He came out occasionally to meet with Jean and I, but we spent the entire day hanging around, first in the rectory, and then out in the town square. It was a very long day, and although we did meet some interesting Haitians in the park, we felt a bit abandoned. Patience, I told myself, this was going to take patience. I am glad I had Jean along with me, we had some great conversations together to pass the time, and the weather was nice up in the high plateau.

The next day at Mass I was introduced to a man named LaFleur Pierrot. He was a handsome tall Haitian man with beautiful green piercing eyes. He seemed well educated, and introduced himself as the supervisor of all the local schools for the Diocese of Hinche. After Mass I spoke with him out in the churchyard, and asked him about the Sacre Coeur School in Cabestor and how it was run: other questions such as that. LaFleur became very guarded and somewhat evasive with his answers finally saying, "You'll have to ask Pè Hermann, he's the pastor."

About that time Hermann came out of the rectory and looked somewhat upset saying with a stern voice that "You need to come in and eat."

At that point LaFleur seemed to scoot off rather quickly. "Hmm." I thought. "I wonder what all that was about."

The breakfast conversation was rather subdued. I talked with Hermann about my desire to speak with LaFleur about the school in Cabestor, and I asked if I could meet with some of the teachers, especially Sonrius. Hermann appeared perturbed, and Pè Bertrand said, "Father Hermann is not happy you were talking to LaFleur or to the other teachers. He is the pastor, and if you have any questions about the schools you need to come to him. As the pastor he is like the mayor and he doesn't like you trying to arrange things without involving him. This has made him upset." There was a seriousness about how Bertrand gave us this advice, and Hermann also showed displeasure on his face.

Again, there was silence. And with all sincerity I apologized to Hermann and Bertrand explaining that this would not have been a problem in the U.S., and I explained that all I was trying to do was have a conversation with LaFleur. I said I was sorry many times, and acknowledged that Hermann was the pastor, and the boss of the parish. I know this now and I will ask before I go out with my own plans. They seemed to be accepting of my apology, and lightened up some.

Jean and I went out around town that afternoon, and of course I took her to Jean Claude's home, but he was not there. His wife told us he was out working on a job in the country. The baby was still growing, now he wore a shirt, but still no pants until potty trained. I once again gave her the family photos we had taken, and she seemed pleased. We sat under the shade tree next to the old dump truck, which was now stripped of its doors and seats from what I could see. After some time I said, "Voye salye Jean Claude pou-m." (Send greetings to Jean Claude for me), and we left.

We ended up back at the rectory where Jean became interested in what the ladies in the kitchen were doing. There was an older woman named Justine who was somewhat heavy set, a liability from working with food all day. She hardly smiled much, and seemed like a no nonsense sort of woman. A younger friendlier woman named Chantal was helping her. Chantal was thin and pretty, with the most beautiful smile; she was a good compliment to Justine. Jean was interested in all the work that was needed to take chicken from walking around the yard, to on your plate. These women spent all day preparing the food we ate. Hermann was making sure we had good meals our entire stay.

While Jean was with Justine and Chantal learning about their kitchen duties, I spent some time with my old friend Roland. You remember, koulev – snake. We played some more word games and watched a turkey that was tied up in the yard.

"Kodenn." Roland said pointing to the turkey. I had never seen a live turkey before: city boy, remember.

About then Tifi came walking into the yard, my little friend had come back again. She was looking for a hand out, and seemed pretty dirty with ripped clothes and shuffling while leaning on her walking stick. She also looked hungry; I thought, "I could give her some bread from inside the rectory." So I brought her a slice. She just held it as if not knowing what to do. I noticed for the first time that her teeth were in really bad shape, with the tops ground down to the core, and all of them short and stained. I had heard about how poor children would eat dirt, or make 'dirt bread' to fill their stomachs, and I wondered if her teeth had been ground down from eating dirt. Finally she put a small piece of bread in her mouth and chewed it slowly. I asked Roland to get me some water and a rag so I could clean the dust off of her. He went and got these things.

As I was getting ready to clean her, Pè Hermann called out in Kreyòl as if to say "Stop this, don't give her a bath." And I complied. I found out from Pè Bertrand that the women bathed her every morning, and afterwards she would just go out and smear dust and dirt all over her body and dress. I guess it is better for Tifi's begging business. Suddenly when I mentioned Tifi it dawned on me. I knew enough Kreyòl to realize that ti is Kreyòl for small, and fi means girl: Tifi just meant 'little girl.' "That's not a name!" I said, "That's just what you all call her. She must have a real name, what's her real name?"

Roland understood and told me. "Rose Carmel name. Li rele Rose Carmel."

Slowly I repeated her name, "Rose Carmel. . . Rose Carmel. So you have a real name." I thought. "That's what I will call you from now on, you are not just any little girl; you are Rose Carmel. Someone gave you that name; someone who loved you enough to name you with such a beautiful name." All of this was going through my mind as this pitiful bone thin, bent over girl who was probably older than her size would suggest, stood there holding her walking stick and half eaten bread. She had trouble chewing it, and she could not even finish the bread before she dropped it, and shuffled off. To where? I never knew.

That evening at dinner, I realized that I was still carrying that $35,000 check with me. I knew eventually that I would have to do something with it. We still had not hit it off with Hermann, but I thought it was time to trust him. I remembered what Ron had said about a public announcement telling the people what we were doing, so I asked Pè Hermann if I could talk briefly to the parish at the Masses Sunday morning. Again he said nothing. This was Haitian code for: "It's better to give no response, than to give bad news."

I was a little perturbed, and was tired of playing the role of patient guest, "Hermann." I interjected, "We're here to visit the parish; people need to know who we are, and why we are here. We didn't come all this way just to leave without telling the parish that we were here." Bertrand translated, and Hermann seemed to reflect on it without responding. So I mentioned, "One of the reasons we are here is to form a bond with the parishioners. We also need to get started on the construction of the school; we need to let the parish know this." Pausing to calm down, I said, "By the way, I have some money so we can get started on the project. I was thinking we should start a Fonkoze account to keep it safe. Have you heard of Fonkoze? What do you think of this?"

Hermann's eyes lit up, "Koman ou konnen Fonkoze?" He asked, amazed that we knew about Fonkoze.

Bertrand explained, "Hermann had helped get the Mirebalais Fonkoze opened when he was pastor there. It's a great organization for the poor."

"Well," I said, "I think it would be good if we could put this money into Fonkoze, and that would give us a way to wire money in the future."

Hermann seemed to like the idea, and Bertrand said that tomorrow we could go open a Fonkoze account in Mirebalais. Hermann seemed surprised at the amount of money I was carrying in my pocket. He asked if we liked the food, and if there was anything else that they could cook for us while we were here.

"I've never had Kodenn here before." I said. And Hermann laughed.

The next day we again found ourselves in Mirebalais, it was usually a busier village than Lascahobas. We parked outside this small cinderblock building with a heavy gate made of thick metal bars, with a large shotgun wielding Haitian man dressed in a black uniform guarding it. The sign said, "FONKOZE: Yon Bank Pou Kore Organizasyonn Yo" (A bank to support local organizations).

We entered and spoke with the manager about opening an account, which he helped us with. Although small, the bank was filled inside and out with peasants making bank transactions. As usual, they all waited patiently. After we were finished, Hermann seemed pleased with having a Fonkoze account, and motioned that he wanted to take us somewhere.

We drove a few miles out of Mirebalais towards Port-au-Prince, and Hermann stopped at a recently built church right off the main road. "This is St. Anne's Chapel." He said. "I built this." There was a sense of pride in what he had accomplished. St. Anne's appeared to be a fairly well built, and a good-sized church. Pè Bertrand explained that this chapel was about to get its own priest and become a parish.

"Pè Hermann is good at getting things built." Bertrand said to Hermann's smiling.

"Well I see that! Great work Hermann." I complimented, as Hermann's eyes sparkled.

We drove back to Lascahobas, stopping in Mirebalais to pick up Venel. It was nice seeing my old friend again; he was coming from a Kiro organizational meeting. Venel and Hermann seemed to get along well, and having Venel in the car seemed to put Hermann at ease.

Later, back at St. Gabriel's, we once again sat down for a shared meal. We prayed, and then Hermann had this mischievous smile on his face. "What's the matter?" I asked.

Hermann uncovered the food and said, "Kodenn!" With a smile.

"What?" I said, looking out into the yard. The turkey wasn't tied up to its spot anymore. "Where's the turkey?" I inquired, somewhat concerned.

"Kodenn mouri pou Tom." Hermann explained. "The turkey die for you."

"No!" I exclaimed, "I was just getting to like the little guy." To which Hermann just laughed like I had never seen him laugh before.

All evening long, Hermann just kept repeating, "Kodenn mouri pou Tom." followed by laughter. This would become our sign.

It was Sunday morning, and time for the big Masses of the week. Jean and I went so that we would at least be visible to the community, and could speak to some of the people afterwards. At the end of the Masses, Pè Hermann did something unexpected. He stood up and gave a somewhat lengthy explanation to his parish telling them about our visit and our mutual project. He then had us stand up to be introduced to the parish. People clapped while Hermann just smiled at us. "That was really nice," I thought. "Thanks Hermann."

After Mass Hermann seemed different, less guarded: almost giddy. He invited Jean and I upstairs onto the covered walkway patio where a small lace covered table was set up surrounded by chairs. Hermann had a bottle of wine, which he was uncorking. On the table was set four wine glasses and a plate of hors d'ovres. A closer look at the plate of hors d'ovres showed them to be large cheese puff snacks laid out individually with toothpicks in each one. Hermann poured a glass of wine for us all, and toasted Bertrand, Jean and myself.

"Thank you for your visit Jean and Tom." Hermann toasted, with his glass raised, "You are always welcome here. From now on, my home is your home. Bondye beni nou."

"Salut!" I responded as we all clinked glasses. We then sat in the shady breeze, on that wonderfully warm Sunday afternoon, chatting and laughing the time away. Something happened that day, I don't know what, but we had formed bonds of respect, trust, and mutual friendship and love for each other. Also, I have to say that those had to have been the most elegant cheese puffs I had ever eaten: one toothpick at a time.

Pè Hermann, Tom, Pè Bertrand. St. Gabriel's Rectory.

Old Sacre Coeur School: Cabestor, Haiti.

Sonrius Jean Baptiste, Director Sacre Coeur School.

11
Cabestor Rising

Men anpil, chay pa lou.

Many hands make the load lighter.

I really needed to learn Kreyòl. Not only to communicate with Hermann, but so that I could learn more about the lives of all the Haitian's I was meeting in and around Lascahobas. Someone told me that to know a people, you need to know their language. I wanted to know the Haitian people.

Pè Hermann was getting things ready to start the school construction, and we decided to try and communicate by phone. St. Gabriel's Parish did not have a phone, but Lascahobas had a Teleco Station we could use to contact each other. Teleco is Haiti's official telephone company, and since most people do not have a phone, they can go to a Teleco Station and pay to use one to call out. A person could also call Teleco and they will have someone in town summoned for them. It was somewhat cumbersome, but it was the best instant communication we could get in Haiti. Many times the phone connection was not working. If I was able to contact Teleco, I had to call back in 30 minutes while they sent a kid out to search the town for my contact. One time I called back only to find out that they summoned the Hermann who sells local lottery tickets and not Pè Hermann. All of this was expensive, and all of this was in Kreyòl.

I took a crash course called "Kreyòl Rapid" given at a retreat house. It was an intensive week of study, and although I did not learn to speak Kreyòl well, I finally understood its grammar rules, and how to put sentences together. Roland only taught me nouns, but that was a start. Afterwards I realized that you could read the book all you wanted, but you really needed to speak with Haitians to learn Kreyòl. I had a hard enough time speaking English.

One day an acquaintance told me of a Haitian man that worked with her who was 'really nice' and a recent immigrant from Haiti. Let's call him Anel St. Yves to protect his privacy. My friend had mentioned my work in Haiti and Anel was interested in meeting me. We set up a meeting, but he did not show. I called and rescheduled, and he finally showed; he seemed a little cautious about who I was and what I wanted. Haitians can be cautious around strangers sometimes, and probably for good reason. Anel is a quiet, intelligent man with a gentle smile and round face. He was very interested in all of my Haiti photos that showed his home country, and he seemed a little homesick. He had been in the United States for less than two years when I met him; his family was still in Port-au-Prince.

Initially Anel had been staying in another Haitian family's apartment until he could find his own place. He had been living in Brooklyn with his Aunt, but did not like the big city. Anel's English was pretty good, and we struck up a friendship; he agreed to help me with my Kreyòl, and I could help him with his English. I spent most of my Saturday mornings at Anel's apartment for our Kreyòl lessons, and he also taught me much about Haitian life, and Haitian proverbs. It became obvious to me that moving from Haiti to the U.S. was not an easy transition.

I had to teach Anel not to trust people, isn't that an odd lesson. At the mall people were always giving him 'free' things, which he thought was amazing, until I would point out the fine print to him. Once he was in a fender bender car accident and was asked by the policeman if he wanted to see a doctor.

"Sure." He said. He was just in an accident, it sounded like a good idea to go see a doctor. Several weeks later while at his apartment he asked me about a bill he received for $350 from the City.

"Anel." I said, "This is for an ambulance ride. Did you take an ambulance?"

"Yes Tom." Anel said sheepishly, as if he were a naughty boy, "They asked me if I wanted to go, so I said yes."

I gave Anel another lesson about the U.S., everything costs you; do not volunteer for anything unless you need it. And always expect a bill. Just about every week there would be another crisis with bills, or something he innocently signed up for or got into. I wondered how other Haitian immigrants were able to survive without someone to help them through the maze of obstacles in their way. He always seemed so sorry, like a little kid who did something wrong. We would work it out, speak some Kreyòl, and then he would make me some Haitian food.

Meeting Anel opened up my eyes to a relatively large underground Haitian community living in the Roanoke area. It was great having that resource for advice, or for the times when I would call Hermann, Anel would be my Kreyòl mouthpiece. I was planning to go back to Haiti to check on the school construction, and I asked about Anel's family in Port-au-Prince. The family lived on Delmas 58, not too far from Visitation House, which is off Delmas 33.

Anel drew me a map to help me find their little house and told me, "When you get to the church, just ask for Madame Jean. They'll point you to my wife."

"Madame Jean?" I said, "This is your wife? Shouldn't I ask for Madame Anel?"

"Well," Anel said, "I'm Jean in Haiti."

Hmmm, I thought, that is interesting. Then I remembered the other week when he was celebrating his birthday he told me that it was 'one of his birthdays.' I did not understand it at the time, and just thought it was a slip of his English.

I inquired, "Anel, didn't you tell me you had two birthdays? And how is it you are Jean in Haiti?"

Anel became somewhat quiet and then told me the story of how he came to the U.S. Anel, whose name was Jean, had a good friend in Haiti who he grew up with. This friend's mother had the chance to immigrate to the U.S. by herself and live in New York City, but the son, whose name was Anel, had to be left behind. Jean and his friend were like brothers, and Jean looked after him while the mother was away trying to bring her son into the U.S. Unfortunately Anel died from an infection while in Haiti. Jean had done everything he could to help, but it was not enough. Even in this tragedy, the mother was very grateful for Jean's help, and wanted to reward him in some way. So Jean took on the identity of his now deceased friend and was able to get his permanent visa to the U.S. under this name. The two men were about the same age, and Haitian, so no one really challenged it. Now Jean is Anel. Haitians will do whatever it takes to get into the U.S. The only other option, one proposed by Haitian President Prèval, was to "Naje pou soti." (Swim to get out.)

"Your secret is safe Anel." I said.

Months later, I found myself back in Port-au-Prince and Visitation House. Ron was still looking tanned from all the work he did with his neighborhood ministries, and he was busy with people coming and going from the house. I had Domo drive me to Delmas 58 to visit Madame Jean and bring her a care package from Anel. Delmas is one of the city's main arteries and is packed with tap-taps, people, and smoky cars and trucks. Domo dropped me off, and was going to run some errands and return for me in an hour. I followed Anel's map down the much smaller street, Delmas 58, and then through the alleyway asking for Madame Jean as I was told. In the back was a narrow passageway lined with the doorways of small living quarters. The passageway opened into a small yard; Madame Jean was waiting there with her four children all dressed up ready to greet me.

We all gave our kisses on the cheek and said our 'bonjou's,' and then we sat and talked. They brought out a big tray on which they served tall glasses of fresh juice on ice. It was all done so formally and elegantly, and the cold juice was a welcome relief from the city heat. They all had so little, but took great pride in dressing cleanly, and being good hosts. Haitians do not have much to give, but I have found that they give what they can: hospitality to strangers. And they give it graciously.

I was then shown their tiny house. It was built out of the cargo box from an old U-Haul type truck, and it had a door cut into the side. This box-house was set up on cinder blocks. Inside were two sets of bunk beds, the mom's bed, a rack of clothes, and an oven. Not much room for movement. They cooked out in the yard, and ate there too. The children were delightful, and included the baby who was born just before Anel left for the U.S. They missed their dad terribly, and Madame was working as a baker of cakes to support the family along with the money Anel would send down. On the way out, I grabbed a hug from each one of them and told them I would bring it back to their dad/husband when I returned to Virginia.

In Lascahobas, Hermann and I struck up our friendship once again over dinner. I continued my Kreyòl lessons with him and Bertrand. I was glad to hear that the construction of the school was underway, but he told me that in order to get a lot of the supplies to Cabestor he would have to build a road out there.

"A road!" I said, "Building a road was not included in our budget."

"Don't worry Tom, I'll show you." He reassured me.

Bertrand told me the story of how Hermann had hired a group of local men, bought them some pickaxes, made some food for them, and paid them the usual daily wage, about a dollar a day, to straighten and widen the trail. Hermann had actually been able to get his car all the way through to Cabestor, much to the joy of the locals who had never seen a car reach Cabestor before. I was told that they all yelled "El Presidente! El Presidente!" as his car rolled up in what must have looked like a royal procession for Cabestor.

"You'll see tomorrow." Hermann said. He then served me an avocado and said, "Tom. Zaboca mouri pou ou." To raucous laughter.

All I could do was smile and shake my head.

At Mass that morning Rose Carmel appeared as before, front and center right during the offertory. As she came shuffling in bent over and leaning on her stick I thought, "She really knows how to make an entrance." It was as if she was announcing to everyone, "I'm here. I'm still here and I will not let you all forget about me." She stood up front for a while, and then slowly made her way down the aisle. She held out her hand while looking up at me with those wanting eyes. I had a few small goudes in my pocket, and I handed her a coin. She took it, put it to her mouth and held it between her lips for a short time while just standing there. Removing the coin, she turned to a child sitting in front of me and handed it to him, and then walked up next to me cuddling by my side like she had done before.

She seemed to be commenting on the coin saying, "I can't eat this. This doesn't sustain me, but what I really need is for you to just hold me for a little while." It was another Rose Carmel moment; after which she stared up at me for some time, and then shuffled her way out the back of the church. I have always felt that she was a special soul.

I saw Venel sitting over to the side, and after Mass we talked. "Tom. I have this idea to help some women in the countryside who have lost their husbands." He went on about his deep desire to help the poor in and around Lascahobas, and wondered if I could help. Reluctantly I said that I could not, but gave him encouragement for the work he was doing. He gave me one of his wide smiles, and looked into my eyes for a while before patting my hand and then departing. Venel was another one of those special people I would run into during my visits.

That afternoon I decided to take a walk around town, and I stopped in to see Sister Laurette and company. They were gracious hosts as before, and served some homemade ice cream before I left; they were all doing fine.

I then walked out of town towards Belladaire, but as I was making my way into the country I noticed that everyone else was coming into town. I was the only one walking out. The sky was a bit cloudy, so I stopped and thought for a while, "Hmmm. I wonder if they know something I don't?" I decided to follow the crowd back into town, and by then people were starting to pick up their pace a bit.

Suddenly it hit. The rain started falling with just a gentle sprinkle, quickly followed by buckets of a heavy tropical downpour. When it rains in Haiti, it really rains hard. I ducked under a covered porch along with a Haitian woman and her son, all of us soaked and smiling at each other. Across the street I noticed a woman in her home waving as if to invite me over. I ran over to see what she wanted.

I was introduced to Estelle Dubuisson, a Haitian-American woman who grew up in Lascahobas, but lived most of her life in Brooklyn, N.Y. A women in her late fifties, Estelle spoke very deliberately as she told me her history. She was a medical technologist, and has been working to help the people of Lascahobas for over twenty years. She told me about all of the projects she had started; but she was most proud of her hospital. "Would you like to see it?" she asked. And once the rain stopped we visited "Hospital Lascahobas."

The hospital was a fairly impressive building, with two operating rooms, some x-ray equipment, examining rooms, beds, and other supplies. I was impressed; she then explained with obvious pride. "There are no doctors or hospitals around Lascahobas. The State inspectors told me that I have the best hospital in this area."

After touring the facility, I asked where the employees were: the doctors and the nurses. She told me how she had very little money to run the hospital, and had to rely on volunteer medical people from the U.S. to come occasionally to operate, and see patients. They charge for services, and unfortunately most people really cannot pay. "It's hard to keep it running. I don't know how I'm going to get the money to keep it running. Even the government can't help me."

So there stood this beautiful facility, but it was useless without people to work it. That seemed to be a recurring theme in Haiti, people build structures, but do not follow through to provide for the project's sustainability. I have been told, "Haiti is the land of broken dreams," because of all the abandoned buildings started with good hopes, but the projects were never sustained. It gave me much to think about. I spent the rest of the day listening to Estelle tell me her stories, and she had a lot of stories.

Morning came, and Hermann loaded up the Land Rover so that we could visit Cabestor. Pè Bertrand was out there already working with the road crew; they were continuing to widen the road so that trucks could carry in supplies. We splashed through the river, which was high from yesterday's rains, and we drove past all the commuters along the county road up the Cabestor Valley. Along the way we stopped at a compound, where an older man with a salt and pepper beard greeted us and talked with Pè Hermann. They seemed to be friends, and he introduced himself to me as Phillip. We shook and he said good-bye with a very husky voice, but an engaging and friendly smile.

When we came to where the end of the road used to be, Pè Hermann said with a proud smile, "Now I show you highway Cabestor." The trail had been widened and graded, and we passed smoothly by in our vehicle.

"This road is amazing!" I exclaimed, to Hermann's chuckles. We passed several gullies and streams that were cut out to allow the car to pass, at one of these streams we meet up with Bertrand and the road crew. There I saw a scene like I have never seen before. Bertrand was directing about twenty-five rough and tumble looking Haitian men wielding large picks. Most of them were shirtless and grimy from the work they were doing. Some wore large rubber boots, and had cigarettes hanging from their mouths. It reminded me of those old photos with groups of miners working the California gold rush. They had just been laying rocks to cover the stream so that cars could pass, and they were getting ready to widen the road up the gully. We stopped to talk and watch them work; the workers then lined up in a row picking at the side of the hill in synchrony like a prison chain gang. They moved to Bertrand's rhythm, it all looked very efficient, and soon they had made good progress. It was just another amazing Haitian moment, what they can accomplish is unbelievable.

"You're building a road Hermann!" I exclaimed awestruck. He again just smiled and laughed at me shaking his head.

The road was passable to Cabestor, but not wide enough yet to allow trucks through. When we arrived, I noticed that the school was out during construction, and only a few local children and adults were around watching. I met the foreman: Pelig. He is a muscular, but wiry man with boundless energy, and he has a very animated face and arm gestures when talking. He has a great sense of humor, and loves to joke with people and his friend Pè Hermann.

Hermann stated. "Pelig built St. Anne's. He is my builder. He can make anything."

Pelig and Hermann talked in Kreyòl about the progress, and showed me around. There was a beautiful rock wall going up and I thought that the school would be made of stone. How beautiful. "No." They said, "That's just the foundation; we'll be building with block."

There was also a man sitting on a pile of gravel wielding a hammer, taking the big rocks, and making them into little rocks. He had a big proud smile on his face, showing me all that he had accomplished. The pride that all the men had in being able to work and get paid was remarkable, understandable, and not unexpected if you think about your own experience.

"Where did you get the stones from?" I asked.

Bertrand explained. "There are stones everywhere in Haiti. When the farmers plow, they hit stone and have to move them. They're in the river, on the trails; people are always walking over them. We paid people for bringing them in."

"This was great," I thought. Then I thought of the symbolism; these stones represented the hardness of life in Haiti, tripping, hitting, and walking over rocks all day long. But now, these symbols of the hardness of their lives have become the foundation of their hope. They have become the foundation of Sacre Coeur School.

Another group of men were working on digging a well in one spot, and planning for a latrine in another. The dirt from these would fill in the foundation. Just watching the school rise up from the ground was very emotional for me, like experiencing the birth of your first child, and watching it grow. "It's really happening." I told Hermann. And I realized what a good building project supervisor he was. I needed Pol's people skills early on, but now Hermann would prove to be invaluable in putting the project together. "Mesi, Pè Hermann. Mwen kontan ampil." I relayed my happiness.

Our last meal together was another special occasion. Justine had cooked a special vegetable dish called legim, which was served over mayi moulen (spiced ground corn and beans). Later they brought out a cake over which we poured Haitian honey. Hermann opened a bottle of vermouth and poured it into special glasses. A toast was made, and words were spoken; but they did not need to be said. Hermann and I were light years ahead of where we had been before. We had a mutual trust, a mutual respect, and a mutual love for each other; we really understood each other. We had built a relationship. It was not written on paper, but it had grown with time and patience.

Road crew building the 'Highway to Cabestor.'

School foundation built on the stones of Haitian life.

12
Jean Claude

Nèg di san fè; Bondye fè san di.

People speak but do not act; God acts but doesn't speak.

Standing in front of the finished Sacre Coeur School in Cabestor during this New Year's dedication ceremony, surrounded by all of these uniformed little waifs, I have a deep sense of contentment, and a feeling of indescribable joy. Taped to the side of the school is an artistically hand written sign that reads:

We are So Happy to
Have you by our side
To Share this
"Great Moment."
Peace to you My Friends.

Sonrius Jean Baptiste, the school's director, has assembled the school children in front of the school for a small ceremony before Pè Hermann's official school blessing. As I stand under the cover of the school's walkway looking out into all the smiling and hope filled faces of the parents and visiting country folk; I cannot help but notice the class of first graders right in front of me. Their uniforms look overly large, not quite fitting, with baggy pants held up with rope, and shirts half-in half-out. These uniforms were probably passed down from big brother or sister. They stand there so small looking up with curious, wanting eyes at this strange visitor. Sonrius directs them to sing a song. So sweetly they sing, the words happy, but their faces and eyes innocent yet tired. These are my children. They are my children as sure as if they were of my flesh. The bond is set; the happy trap has been closed forever, ensnaring my soul within love's jaws.

Sonrius made some statements of thanks on behalf of himself, the teachers, the students, and their families. I was then handed a gift from one of the little students. They were a basket of oranges, and a gift-wrapped box of something (I was later told they were eggs, but not before a few broke). More clapping and another song was sung. I wanted to repay the gift, so I took three of the oranges and juggled for them all. They seemed surprised, and they liked this little show. Hermann then walked around the school baptizing it with water sprinkled with branches of leaves, while the white robed dancers followed.

After this, the Festival, 'Fèt-la,' began. I saw Jean Claude and his wife, with their oldest son Claudzi. We chatted and he went off, but not until he gave me one of his rib-crushing hugs. Note to self: take a deep breath before he hugs you next time. I ran into Phillip whom I had met at Mass, and on the road to Cabestor last time we drove here. He is the friend of Pè Hermann with the salt and pepper beard. He wanted me to take another photo of him and his beautiful Haitian wife. He spoke words of gratitude with his somewhat gravelly voice, and then went off to join the Fèt-la.

A group of the teachers approached me during the festivities, and they brought along Pè Wilcoxson the new associate priest to translate for them. "They would like to speak with you." Pè Wilcoxson told me. So we went aside and Pè Wilcoxson continued, "They would like to tell you how grateful they all are for the new school, and they say 'thank you.' But they have a problem." Wilcoxson translated "They have not been paid for a very long time."

"You aren't getting paid!" I repeated somewhat incredulously.

"No." Wilcoxson continued translating, "Pè Hermann only gives them some bananas or food, and lets their children go to school here. He only gives them a few dollars when he gets some money, but it isn't very much."

"Wow!" I said, "I thought the kids paid tuition or something. I thought you ran the school here and just needed a new building. I helped you get your school building. No one pays the teachers?"

"The families and children don't have anything out here." Wilcoxson told me, "They don't have money for school. They can barely find the money to pay for their uniforms. The teachers were wondering if you could help get money to pay their salaries?"

Again: pause. Now with mouth open and jaw dropped I spoke. "What! I just built you a school. Am I supposed to pay the salaries now too?" Closing my eyes, and shaking my head slightly back and forth, I thought about this. Slowly I responded. "We'll see what we can do."

"Thank you!" They all said with broad smiles and animated handshakes. "N'a we pita." They said while waving and walking off. After this, I started looking for the man with the kleren: Haitian moonshine. And at this point I did not care what was floating in it.

That evening back in Lascahobas I spoke with Hermann about the situation the teachers asked me about. "Yes." He said, "We have the eight teachers in Cabestor, but we also work with four teachers that have a little school up in the mountains on Mon Michel. Since they work together, it would be good if you could find money for the salaries of all twelve of these teachers."

"How much do teachers get paid here?" I asked, bracing for the news.

"I think if you can get them $35 per month, that would be good." Hermann said in Kreyòl.

"Oh" I said, "That doesn't seem too bad; we'll see what can be done." Being that it was now past midnight, and a busy day we easily went off to sleep.

Before we left for home, I had the idea of taking the students' individual photos. We lined them up, while Hermann wrote down their names. "I think we'll try to 'adopt' these kids in the U.S. to get money for the school." I told him. Hermann just laughed, amused by my idea. I realized that these children had never had their pictures taken, and did not know how to smile for a photo. They had perplexed looks on their faces from watching the whole camera thing, which was foreign to them. They only smiled after they were released from their photographic bondage, and were set free to run off.

Back home in Salem, we had our own new pastor, Father Jeremiusz Sojka; we just call him Fr. Remi for short. He came to us via Poland, and Our Lady of Perpetual Help was his first parish as pastor. Even though he was busy with the plans for our own church's construction and renovation, he let me continue to beg for money to help pay the teachers salaries. People liked having photos of a child so that they could put a face to the project, which was far away and hard to grasp. Fr. Remi allowed me to speak to the parish from time to time, so that as a community we could slowly become one with our adopted Haitian community. It's hard building a relationship with a people so far away. I continued inviting people to make the journey to Haiti and visit the parish, but people were busy. Many people were afraid to go to Haiti for fear of violence or illness. So I continued to beg, and ask for money for our little brothers and sisters in Cabestor.

As I prepared to make another trip to Lascahobas, I made a call to Hermann through Teleco with the help of my Haitian friend Anel St. Yves. Hermann had been receiving the money through Fonkoze, and this system was working well. I told him that I would like to visit Mon Michel when our group comes, and he said that he could arrange that for me. He also said that he would drive us to Lascahobas from Port-au-Prince, so that we did not have to hire Thimothè. That would be a treat.

I arrived at Visitation House with our group, which included Mary, her son Timothy, and teenage daughter Elizabeth. Hermann drove us through the city, up Mon Kabrit, and we arrived safely in Lascahobas. The sights and images of Haiti were just too much for Elizabeth, and she went straight to her room passing up the welcome dinner. The plan was to rest tomorrow, and climb Mon Michel the day after. We prepared ourselves for a long trip up there.

The next day I took the group around town for the tour. Rose Carmel had already made her appearance at morning Mass; afterwards we stopped at Jean Claude's house. His wife was there, as was his oldest son Claudzi. Although happy to see me, they had a sad serious look on their faces. "Ki-sa pwoblem?" I asked them.

Claudzi told me, "Papa pa la. Li nan prizon."

"Your dad's in prison!" I repeated, very shocked. Apart from his hugs, Jean Claude was the most easygoing, gentlest man I knew. "Why is he in prison?" I pressed them in Kreyòl.

"Politik. Pwoblem politik." Was all Claudzi could tell me as he hung his head downward in sadness for his missing father.

I gave my condolences saying, "Mwen triste ampil pou nou." Afterwards we spent some time listening to their story as we sat under the yard's large shade tree.

I could not believe that news. We left with the knowledge that Claudzi and his friend would be accompanying us to Mon Michel tomorrow. Walking through town we stopped at St. Gabriel's school to visit Sr. Laurette and the other nuns. I was always lifted up by their joyful smiles and laughter, and we never left without hospitality. Today they were serving je kashiman, a special Haitian tropical fruit juice. It is a milky juice that has a slight sweet taste as well as some tartness to it: very different, very good.

I advised the Sisters, "We're going to visit Mon Michel tomorrow." much to their shock.

"You can't go to Mon Michel!" They exclaimed. "It's too hard. You'll die if you try to walk there. We've never gone to Mon Michel."

"Well," I thought, "That's not a great recommendation." But I asked, "Haitians go there. If they can get to Mon Michel, we should be able to."

We left after being escorted to the schoolyard gate, and sent off with the Sisters smiling faces, while being serenaded to their harmonious "Good-bye."

The next day, before we left for Mon Michel, I spoke with Hermann about Sr. Laurette's concerns with us going up the mountain. He laughed and said, "It is difficult, but I take you a good way."

We all drove to Mirebalais along with Claudzi and his friend. We then took the Highway north towards Hinche, and stopped on the side of the road to catch the trail. About a half-mile into our walk, we met up with some men with mules, and we mounted clumsily to the amusement of the Haitians walking by. The trip up was through rolling hills, mostly grassy with scattered fields of grain, banana trees, and gardens. Small children who were accustomed to the trip were just scooting by us even though they were walking without any shoes.

We would stop along the way to say hello to people sitting by some of the groupings of small houses. Occasionally they would offer us fresh coconut milk to drink. Often they would tell us, "Coconut milk is good if you're sick." Good advice, I'm sure.

The climb became much steeper towards the top of the mountain. At the top, the trail moved over large smooth rocky outcroppings. These slippery surfaces were usually near the edge, and I really would have felt more secure on my own feet, rather than trusting the mule. Hermann just laughed at my expressions of concern saying, "Tom, trouble."

As we approached St. Michel's Chapel, the gardens all became a little greener, and the trees a little denser. The spot on the mountain where the chapel was built was picked because of the streams and springs nearby. Finally we came upon a flat grassy churchyard filled with people waiting for Pè Hermann, and for Mass to begin. The chapel was impressive, especially given the fact that it was so far up on this mountain, far away from any roads, and yet there it stood, this beautiful stone church. Another Pere Blot project I was told, built from stones taken from all around this mountain.

Once I unfolded my legs off the mule, and relearned how to walk, I wanted to stay there and talk with all the people who were anxiously awaiting us, but Hermann wanted to get on with things. I am sure he was thinking about the trip back. After a short water break, people were directed inside, and the service began. Pè Hermann is only able to get out to these chapels once every three months, so it is a very special occasion when he can finally visit. And it is very infrequent to get visitors like us.

It was another incredible celebration with the children dancing, the drums beating, and the choir's strong voices singing. I always find it so beautiful, especially the little girls dancing in bare feet with hands and eyes gesturing towards heaven in praise and thanksgiving.

Outside after Mass I had the chance to talk with people. It is a great thing to be able to encourage someone just by being present to them. One older student told me that people see the United States as a wonderful place, and they found it incredible that someone would leave the U.S. to visit Haiti: especially way out here.

We spent the rest of the afternoon hanging out in the churchyard with people eating and socializing, another lazy Haitian Sunday. The students were in their uniforms, and we took some of their photos for 'adoption' as well. They just all looked so scruffy and forgotten. When you took a group picture they would all push to get in it. Their faces and eyes seeming to say, "Oh look at me, pay attention to me. I want to be special, I want to be noticed too."

I spoke with the four teachers, and they told me that the school now had 250 students. They have been meeting in the church, which although not ideal, is at least dry. They would like to have a school up on Mon Michel, but they know how difficult it is to bring materials up here for construction. I then thanked them for all the help they give to the students, "Mesi ampil pou tout ed ou bay elev-yo."

The view from up top was spectacular. The vista revealed the entirety of the Central Plateau out to Hinche. You could see the National Highway #3 going up along Lake Peligre leading past Cange. And of course there was the lake itself, framed by those Haitian mountains and cliffs: all of it breathtakingly beautiful. It would have been great to stay longer, but it was getting late and we needed to get back.

Thankfully Claudzi and his friend carried up water for us; I decided to walk down with them rather than ride the mule. They were typical teenagers, and we walked fast and made good time to the trailhead where we waited for the group. While waiting, there were people curious to talk with us, and a group of little Haitian children who were really scared of the blan. As much as I tried to slowly approach them, the more fearful they became. A quick movement, and they would run off screaming. This was easy entertainment for the crowd.

In Lascahobas I walked Claudzi back to his home, luckily he had learned his dad's trade and would be working as a carpenter's apprentice to support his family. He had no idea when his dad would be back. I missed Jean Claude, he always made me smile, and his energy recharged me. Claudzi's little brothers and sisters where all playing in the yard on that abandoned dump truck which now had its engine and axels missing. "What's going on with the truck Claudzi?" I asked.

"My dad found it abandoned, and we pushed it home. We've been selling it little by little for money." Claudzi explained in Kreyòl.

"I see." I said. Then I wished them all good night, "Bon swa tout moun. Pase bon nwit."

Back at the rectory, Mary and her family were recuperating up in their room. Hermann offered me a Prestige beer, which I never refused. As we sat talking, a priest friend of Hermann's stopped by and he arose so that they could greet each other. I followed, and noticed a unique custom as they greeted. The men touched each other's foreheads together and made a slight rolling motion. When it was my turn to greet the priest I did likewise, and got a slightly perplexed look from the visitor. After a short visit with us, the priest was off.

"What was that head thing about?" I asked Hermann.

"That is a special greeting for Haitian priests. When you did it too, he thought you were a priest, but you're not Haitian. It's ok." Hermann reassured me. Then laughing, "Trouble. Tom trouble." I am always up for a new experience, but didn't know I was joining the priesthood.

Hermann and I talked about our visit to St. Michel's School, and how the student's faces looked worried, and not lively like I think of children's faces. He told me that this was because they were hungry; typically they only eat about one or two meals per week. I could not believe this, so I rechecked the Kreyòl with Wilcoxson, but he told me that this was true. They might eat a banana, or chew on sugar cane, and sometimes their mom's would give them salt water because it would make them thirsty and they would drink more water to fill their stomachs. I just could not fathom going days without eating, especially while walking up and down those mountains. How do they do it?

"Hermann, what can we do about this. The kids can't listen to the teachers if they're listening to their stomachs." I pleaded.

"Tom. We can make them beans and rice." Hermann replied, now more serious in tone. "I can get women to cook the food, but we need money to buy it."

"Hermann, I don't know how we're going to do this, but hand me another Prestige and I'll work on it." We both clinked bottles and laughed one of those 'I'm fatigued and my brain is stressed,' laughs. We laughed until we cried.

Jean Claude, his wife, and his family in the yard.

Cabestor Valley, looking towards Lascahobas.

Pè Hermann if front of the new Sacre Coeur School.

13
Ivan the Terrible

Kay koule twompe soley, men li pa twompe lapli.

The leaky roof can fool the sun, but it can't fool the rain.

Salem, Virginia is a great little town. I love returning here with its mountains and the community emphasis on children and education. People here seem to understand why the Haitians have this same emphasis. I was talking to some of my friends about where the project was at this point. We have the Sacre Coeur School in Cabestor, and we are paying twelve teacher's salaries at Sacre Coeur and St. Michel School on Mon Michel. Recently the beans and rice lunch program began as well. It's not easy finding money to pay for school construction, but it's much easier than asking for money over and over again to pay the intangibles like salaries and food. There is a sort of 'giving fatigue' that starts to settle in with even the most charitable people when they are asked over and over to give for these intangibles. But these intangibles are what sustain the project.

This question of sustainability kept popping up in my mind, and I thought of Estelle Dubuisson and her empty Hospital Lascahobas. I continued to meet with my friend Anel St. Yves for Kreyòl lessons, and he was always great about giving me encouragement. "Tom, for what you are doing, all of Haiti thanks you. I thank you too." He would say. He recently moved into a smaller apartment, and was saving money to bring his family and four children over from Haiti. We started paperwork for both his U.S. citizenship, and for the travel visas for his family. With every new form or paperwork we had to fill out, there was money required. Just when we thought we were getting closer, there was another request for more information, or we were told, "New visas are on hold because of 9-11." and so on.

We had worked on this for years, and the bureaucracy was confusing to me even though I am a professional with good English skills. I do not know how a foreigner could navigate through it all. It is as confusing as filing your tax return: times five. Anel and I were getting very frustrated with the whole process, and there was a time when I wanted to stop. Anel was working 2-3 low paying jobs to support himself, his family including their school expenses, and for the application fees. Even with these jobs, I still had to help him pay the bigger expenses.

Anel and I talked about the schools, and he told me, "Tom. Fr. Hermann is going to ask you to build a school on Mon Michel; I know he will."

I knew this too, now that Sacre Coeur was up and running. I would have to talk with Hermann about this on my next trip. It will be hard raising money for a new school while keeping the other schools running. I made plans to go down in September 2004 with a young man who had traveled with me to Haiti on previous trips; his name is Justin Pendarvis. He had just finished his Masters of International Public Health, I believe he chose this field because of his experiences in Haiti. I found him to be a very thoughtful and caring young man. Like his dad, John Pendarvis, Justin has been gaining knowledge and experiences trying to build a career that would combine both his heart and his head. His dad John advised me early on in the project regarding fund raising. Justin was flying down from Boston, and we planned to meet in Miami.

People, who know the Caribbean, know that September is hurricane season; and 2004 was one of the most costly, and the deadliest hurricane seasons on record. It also holds the record for the most named hurricanes (five) hitting one state (Florida) in a single season. I was watching this weather activity before our trip, but I knew that somehow I would get there safely. Justin was not so sure and kept calling me to make sure I was still going. I was, but I told him he was free to back out if he was uncomfortable; he came anyways.

Ten days before I left Virginia, a giant storm, Hurricane Ivan was making its way through Grenada, Jamaica, and the Cayman Islands wreaking havoc. It had worked its way through the Gulf and was swinging around heading northeast into the southern U.S. Gulf Coast the day before I left. In Roanoke, the weather was dark and cloudy the morning I was to leave, still we were cleared for take off. On our flight south we passed through the massive band of clouds stretching to the west of us that was Tropical Storm Ivan. I remember thinking that I had just gotten out of its way in time. Just one hour after we took off all of the area flights were grounded.

That same week, Hurricane Jeanne was coming through the Atlantic and heading right for the Island of Hispaniola: home to the Dominican Republic and Haiti. I saw the weather reports on Jeanne the day before; although it was coming from the east towards Hispaniola, these storms can go anywhere. When we left Miami, CNN showed Jeanne right over the spine of Hispaniola traveling west, and crossing into Haiti.

Just before take-off, Jeanne was riding the north edge of Haiti, and I was optimistic that the flight could squeeze by. We left Miami flying into clear Florida weather, but as we approached Haiti I could see this giant, thick black bank of clouds just to the east of us as we flew over Haiti. Its top formed a black expansive plane, but the dark storm reached down touching the land and sea. It was staying on the northern edge of Haiti and I could only imagine what was happening on the ground. Port-au-Prince was clear, with blue skies when we landed.

We spent the night with Ron Voss at Visitation House. That evening it became dark, the wind picked up, and the temperature dropped about 15 degrees. Although we had some rain and wind, it never really was that bad, and by morning the storm had passed. I felt like I had literally threaded the needle, passing two hurricanes side-to-side.

Pè Hermann met us at Ron's for our trip to Lascahobas, but arrived with a friend of his from Port-au-Prince. "Where's your car?" I asked.

"It's broken," Hermann said.

I recalled on the last trip how the Land Rover kept overheating the whole drive into town. We had to stop every chance we had to pour water over the engine to cool it off, finally having to push it out of the way on Delmas 33 just before getting to Visitation House. "The water pump is too expensive; we'll take a tap-tap to Lascahobas." Hermann suggested.

"A tap-tap! All the way back?" I repeated, and then after thinking about it "Sure, I'm game, let's go." Justin and I were then driven to a side market on a back street near the center of town. It was late afternoon; we made our way past vendors picking up the scraps of their vegetables, meat, and hardware they had been selling. Hermann asked where the Lascahobas 'bus' was. We were directed to the third covered cargo truck on the right. "We're taking a kamyon! At least it's not filled with bananas as we head back." I commented.

We climbed into the covered bed of the kamyon, there were about ten other tired appearing Haitians carrying supplies they had purchased in town: chairs, a bed, some shoes, and sacks of things. We looked for the best place to sit; all the good spots were already taken: the tire, the sacks, and the ledge against the cab's back window. I was left leaning against one of the metal bars. "This should stabilize me." I thought.

It was evening when we left, so the air was cool, and the wind felt good against us after the long hot Port-au-Prince day. It was always hotter in the city, than up in the mountains. I spoke with some of the Haitian passengers in Kreyòl, and told them about our work. They were grateful, and told me they have never ridden in a kamyon with a blan before. It was a long and bouncy, jarring, back banging ride. For me it was just a new experience, but for the Haitians, this is daily life. I remembered my times at the Haitian clinic when men would tell me, 'they hurt all over.' I was beginning to understand why. By the time we arrived in Mirebalais for a stretch break, it was dark, and my back was imprinted by the stabilizer bar.

I watched Pè Hermann ride with us in the bed of that kamyon; he talked to the people and asked them about their lives. He was wearing his collar, so they knew he was a priest. I just had so much respect for him; this was a man of the Church out with the poor, walking along with them. I developed a great admiration for Hermann on that trip, and I was glad to be working along side such a man.

When we arrived at the rectory, Bazilo, Hermann's grounds keeper, met us to carry our bags. Bazilo is a strong, dark, Haitian country man with wrinkled facial features, and a simple looking smile. He was one of Hermann's parishioners from his former parish. When Bazilo's wife died during childbirth, Hermann gave him a job helping out at his parishes. I noticed that Bazilo was carrying our bags back without any shoes on, just the thick soles of his feet. He welcomed us with, "Byenveni Lascahobas Msye Tom." We quickly went to bed; after a long hard trip like this, I did not notice the dogs barking, the cocks crowing, or the church bells ringing.

Justin and I had a nice rest, and after breakfast Hermann had some errands to take care of, and we were free to explore for the day. "Justin." I asked. "Would you like to canoe across the lake?" By the look on his face, he seemed ready to go. Justin and I walked out of town and I tried to remember where Pè Pol had taken us years ago. We finally arrived there, and hired the young men to take us across the flooded river. The memories of my first trip with Pol came back, but this time the experience was not as foreign to me. I was able to use my Kreyòl to get us there and back, I felt connected to the people, and to this beautiful land. As I looked out over the water, at the green mountains framed by the blue sky, I feel more at ease, and in some ways more at home here; I do not know why.

Back in Lascahobas that afternoon we went to see my old friend Jean Claude; I wondered if he was back from prison. We entered the yard under the shade tree with the partially disassembled truck, but there were no chairs, no family, and the house was closed up. I walked over to another house where Claudzi had been working as a carpenter's apprentice. There were two 'bos chapantye,' or carpenters with Claudzi helping to finish some chairs and a table they were working on. After some introductions and greetings I asked Claudzi where his family was. The workers understood my Kreyòl well enough, and put on somber faces; after this they stopped working telling Claudzi they would be back in a little while. Claudzi and I were alone outside in the small work-yard sitting on one of his newly fashioned chairs. I could tell Claudzi was bothered by something. "Claudzi. Ki kote papa-ou? Where's your dad?"

Claudzi told me he was still in prison, and that he had visited him there. Jean Claude was getting along well because he had made friends with the jailers; still he was suffering because his wrists and ankles were chained together in irons. He has not been able to take them off since he had been put there. His dad was really missing his family. Claudzi started tearing some when he talked about this. "He must miss you and your mom; he's been gone a year now."

Claudzi's eyes became red and now welled up. With a tearful frown he looked at me and cried softly, "Manman. Li te mouri."

"What! Your mom died! Oh Claudzi, I'm so sorry. How?" I asked never expecting this; she was a young woman in her thirties.

"Li te gen infeksyon nan janm. Li te pi malad genyen lafyev. Mouri pandan nwit." He told me about the leg infection that got worse and worse without care, until she died in the night with a high fever. He had visited his father to tell him this news; the jailers said Jean Claude did not eat for several weeks afterwards. This was his third wife to die, the first with dysentery, his second wife during childbirth. Life for women in Haiti is precarious.

Claudzi needed to be held for a few minutes until the men came back for work. He was not a teenager anymore; he went from teen, to being the provider for the home, to the parent, all in one year. His siblings were staying with their aunt while waiting for their dad's return.

That evening as Hermann and I sat out in the churchyard under the night sky, somehow the sky seemed darker than I had remembered it before. Still there was a familiarity to the stars. When I looked up, I realized that these were the same stars that I could see from home. Why did they seem different? Probably because I was here in Haiti. So it's not what you are looking at that makes things appear different, but it's from where you are standing. Being in Haiti, and standing here with my Haitian friends, has made me see things differently.

I spoke with Hermann about Jean Claude, he was aware of the whole situation. Hermann had arranged for Claudzi to get work as an apprentice, and Hermann had accompanied Claudzi to visit and to speak with Jean Claude in prison.

Here is what they learned. A little over a year ago there was an ambush along the road to Belladere outside of Lascahobas; a judge by the name of Christophe Lozama was murdered. This crime was obviously a high profile event, blamed on former Duvalier army members: Lame san manman (The Motherless Army). Suspects were rounded up, arrested, and imprisoned in the Lascahobas Jail across from St. Gabriel's. Months later, while they were awaiting trial, a group carried out a successful jailbreak releasing these suspects.

President Aristide's administration then rounded up anybody who was associated with anti-Aristide activity in the area. Jean Claude, although not involved, was friends with people from this group and he was rounded up with the rest. That was about one year ago; since then there have been no charges filed, and no trial scheduled.

The next morning after breakfast, Justin and I sat out in the churchyard talking about our visit so far. Rose Carmel came in to sit next to us, and I told Justin to go get her a slice of bread to eat. She just sat on the bench next to us slowly eating while continuing to stare up at us with her probing eyes. She fingered the wooden cross I was wearing, and so I gave it to her, putting it around her neck. Rose Carmel sat there for a time until she finally shuffled off down the street.

Later, Venel passed by. He heard we were in town and wanted to stop by and say hello. He was busy with a project trying to start a photocopy business. We said good-bye, and he went off promising to return with a letter for Jean Denton.

We spoke with Hermann about a trip to Cabestor, but because of all the storms, the road they had built was washed out and the path was too muddy. I asked Hermann about the progress at Sacre Coeur School; he said that they had converted the old school into a kitchen where women were cooking the beans and rice over an open fire in large pots. The price of rice and beans increases with every political crisis, Herman asked me to find more money for the food since prices have quadrupled. Also, the teachers were asking for a raise in pay so that they could afford this food for their families; their salaries have more than doubled since we started. The amount needed to sustain the schools kept rising, and Hermann also asked me if we could start thinking about building that school on Mon Michel.

"Hermann." I pleaded, "I'm having trouble finding the money for the salaries, and beans and rice; I can only ask people so many times for money. Although they need a school on Mon Michel, meeting in the church works pretty well for now, and without the money to continue paying their salaries, there is no school. Teachers teach children, the school is only the tool they use."

Hermann listened, and knew this as well. "Mwen konnen sa-a. Ki-sa nap fè?" What are we going to do? He asked.

"I have an idea," I continued. "Let's have another series of fund raising dinners, but this time invest the money into the stock market and use the interest to fund the salaries. We'll start a trust fund as a way to invest for the future of the schools." Hermann smiled, he liked the idea; we would work on it when I got back.

That afternoon some young men came in to tell Hermann that they had heard some bad news. There was flooding in the eastern coastal city of Gonaives, and they heard that 250 people were killed. I could not believe this, and I told Hermann that we passed by Hurricane Jeanne on our way into Haiti. Throughout the day people were coming in to update Hermann about the news they were hearing about the tragedy. Soon it was 1,000 Haitians killed, then 2,000, finally as many as 3,000 Haitians were reported washed away in the night. The ground was already saturated because of past storms and rain, so when Jeanne came through there was nowhere for the water to go.

That night the rains rushed down the mostly treeless mountains, broke through the earthen rice field dams that lined the rich Artibonite River valley, and suddenly and unexpectedly washed away all of the little huts along the way until it swept through the coastal city of Gonaives at the mouth of the Artibonite River. People were just washed out to sea, and this city of 400,000 was still underwater according to reports.

Haitians were so saddened by this news, how much tragedy and bad news can a people take. They were saying that even God was punishing Haiti, but God did not put up those rickety huts by the river. God did not cause all the trees to be sold for hardwoods. God did not put Haitians into the situation of poverty that they are in; we did that as a people. Whether by omission or commission, we as a world community participated, and we need to change our indifference.

It was a sad day, added onto an already somber trip. The bad news was soon to change; Pè Pol came to visit. I had not seen him in a very long time, "Ki-sa anba bra ou-la Tom?" Pol said with a large smile.

"Zouti-m map pote." I faithfully replied. This was our sign. It was from a dialogue on one of my Kreyòl study tapes that Pol found funny. "What's under your arm? It's some tools I'm carrying." Is all that it means, but every time we meet Pol will ask me our secret question. It's silly, but it seems to connect us to our past. It was great seeing him, with his broad smile, deep basso voice and laugh. We embraced, and reconnected. Pol was always so energetic and upbeat.

We spoke some Kreyòl, and he laughed telling me, "Now you are a Haitian: Ayisyan blan." I asked him about his new parish in Belladere, and he told me how poor it was being so close to the border with the Dominican Republic. "I am making the best of it." He said, "When I was visiting you and Fr. Gregory, he had a sign on the wall of my room, 'Dance wherever you may be'. That's what I'm doing in Belladere." And he made a dancing movement while smiling.

Pol was visiting because he had heard that I was in town; I always wondered how news traveled so fast in Haiti without phones or e-mail. Thimothè was also in Belladere with three visitors from Pol's twinned parish in Virginia. "This is great!" I said, "Could you ask Thimothè to give us a ride back, Hermann's car died."

"I will ask him, they are leaving tomorrow." Pol replied. We had a meal together, with Hermann enjoying his visit with Pol as well. You could see their friendship, and their bond of shared experiences as Haitian priests. That evening, Justin and I got ready for our return trip in the morning.

Thimothè arrived the next day with the folks from Norfolk, Virginia; Bazilo loaded up the Land Rover, and we said good-bye. When we got to Mirebalais, Thimothè decided to take the route through the Artibonite valley. This was partially because of all the rains; the road down Mon Kabrit was muddy, while the valley road is paved. We were also curious to see what the flooding from the night before looked like.

The Artibonite valley is beautiful. Thimothè told us that at one time it was called the 'Breadbasket of the Caribbean' because it produced enough rice to feed all of Haiti, as well the other Caribbean countries. Unfortunately with the influx of cheaper subsidized rice from the U.S. starting in the mid 1980's, production has dropped off, making Haiti reliant on foreign sources of rice. When disasters like this hit, Haiti does not have the infrastructure to feed their people.

The river was high, but we did not notice much damage. As we approached St. Marc, the coastal city just south of Gonaives, we saw an escorted convoy of Croix Rouge (Red Cross) trucks bringing food to the area. Thimothè explained that after dropping off the rice, they would use the trucks to carry the dead bodies back, cutting down on disease. Seeing that many large trucks was a gruesome reminder of the number of dead.

We had no trouble getting back to Visitation House, and we caught up on some of the news from Ron. Remember, we had only heard word of mouth news since we had no access to TV or Radio. "You better e-mail your folks back home," Ron told us, "With the news on CNN they'll probably think you all are dead by now."

It was quite the news item for the next few days, and people had been calling my wife to see if I was OK, or if she had heard from me. Her usual response was that, "I will only worry if they call me with news, until then, there is not much I can do but just wait." We did send a reassuring e-mail back home.

Ron was sending Domo to the airport to pick up a young, American woman who the U.N. had helicoptered out of Gonaives. Justin and I met up with Nellie when she arrived at Visitation House, obviously frazzled and a bit shaken up. She was a 22 year-old recent college graduate looking to become a photojournalist. Her editor had sent her to Gonaives a few weeks earlier on her first assignment; it was supposed to be an easy human-interest story about life in a Haitian orphanage. Little did she know that she would be thrust right in the middle of the biggest story of that week. She had her digital camera, and Internet ready laptop right there at the scene, and her editor instructed her, "Take as many photos as you can, we need photos of what happened."

I thought. "What an opportunity for a new photojournalist to find herself in."

Nellie did take some photos, and she talked to some people, but her humanity got the best of her. "I just couldn't stay there and take any more pictures." Nellie explained in tears, "I've never seen anything like this, all the bodies, the crying children, the mud and water, the people trapped on their roofs. I had to get out even though my editor begged me to keep sending photos. So when I saw the U.N. helicopter, I asked them to fly me out."

I guess dealing with the reality of life that one finds at the end of their viewfinder is not something a person learns in college. After this experience Nellie may reconsider her line of work. I was grateful to have Justin along, because he was her age and a kind and patient young man; he sat and talked with her the rest of the day. This seemed to calm her nerves quite a bit.

Hurricane Jeanne would continue to give us trouble, it was now over Miami and blocked our flight out of Haiti. We were lucky enough to get a flight to New York thanks to the help of a Haitian man at the airport, and we made it safely home.

Whether the final count was 2,500 or 3,000; a lot of Haitian families were broken up, or completely lost overnight from this hurricane. More would die from the aftermath: hunger and water borne diseases. I never heard what happened to Nellie, or if she continued in photojournalism. In the end it was probably better that she connected in a human way with the suffering of the Haitian people rather than 'just performing her job.' She was present to the reality of Haiti, and she suffered in solidarity along with the people there. I know that for myself, sharing an experience, and forming a relationship is a greater long-term motivator than just having an immediate emotional reaction to a photo or a news story. Think about this. With all the concerns that people had for Haiti at the time; where is that help today?

Bazilo.

Beans and Rice lunches, Sacre Coeur School.

14
Venel Lamay

Bel anteman pa di paradi.

A beautiful funeral does not guarantee heaven.

The CNN reports on the devastation to Haiti that was caused by Hurricane Jeanne were quite graphic. Although the reality for me on the ground was not as bad, it was difficult for my wife Leah to watch these reports while I was down there. I had not realized before how hard it was for her to stay behind not knowing how I was, or what was happening to me while I was in Haiti. Leah knew how important this project in Haiti was for me and to the Haitian children she had met, so she never questioned my leaving each time. In many ways it's harder to stay behind taking care of all the daily jobs of life, while your husband is off on his adventures to 'save the world.' This is love, and without her support, I could not have continued going to Haiti. Personal visits to Haiti are key to moving a project like this forward, and with that comes just a little risk.

During this last visit I realized that I needed to get serious about planning for the sustainability of this project. I needed to start a trust fund so that we could invest in the future of these schools. I knew nothing about trust funds, so I decided to learn more. The first person I asked was Justin's dad, John Pendarvis who directed me to The Foundation for the Roanoke Valley. Although they were involved in regional charitable work, they helped me to understand how to set up a trust.

Then, with the help of the Diocese of Richmond I was able to write up a trust fund document outlining how the money would be used. Finally I spoke to a friend of mine, Jim Laub, who works as an investment advisor; he agreed to help with the investment aspects of the fund. Jim took the time to advise me on how best to invest the money safely, and he has continued to help manage the O.L.P.H. Haiti Trust Fund. Once the document was approved, I put some money into the trust fund myself to prime it. The trust qualified for 501(c)3 tax-exempt status through our church.

With the trust fund all set; all I needed now was more money. It seems to always come down to money. It was time to ask people for donations again at some fundraising dinners. I organized one with people from the Rotary Club of Salem, and that started the fund going. Several other dinners were organized where I not only asked for, but also agreed to match all of the bigger donations. At that time my medical practice was doing well, so I figured that it was time for me to start investing towards the future of this Haiti project.

People were motivated by the fact that I was putting some of 'my own flesh' into the project, and that I was paying the operating expenses so that 100% of their gifts were going to the Haitian children. All of these factors, along with the stories about the lives of the Haitian people, motivated donors to give. Most people have generous hearts, and want to help; they just need to be assured that their gifts will be used wisely and honestly.

The original trust fund was enough to pay the teacher's salaries in Cabestor and Mon Michel, but the project was growing. I learned that the school on Mon Michel, which started with four teachers, was now so popular that it was up to over 300 students and eight classrooms. Each teacher was teaching two classes simultaneously, so we decided to hire a fifth teacher. All of these factors, along with the rise in teachers' salaries, and the rising price of food, meant that we would have to double the trust fund. And we still needed to ask for the beans and rice money.

Still, the trust fund took the pressure off of worrying about many of the ongoing operating expenses, so I started preparing for the building of a schoolhouse on Mon Michel. I had really tapped all of my resources for donors, so I decided to just save for the school construction myself. Money was put aside until I had enough for another school, this time St. Michel on Mon Michel.

The time came for another visit to St. Gabriel's in Lascahobas. I was not able to visit the Sacre Coeur School in Cabestor last time because of weather, and I was really looking forward to another visit. Once again Jean Denton was coming down, as was my daughter Rachel who had never been to Haiti. My oldest daughter Ryann had already visited several times in the past with us, as well as with a group she organized from college. I felt it was important for my children to see what Haiti and its people were like first hand.

Rachel had the chance to meet Ron Voss at Visitation House who greeted us with, "Blessed are you among women Tom," since I always seemed to bring groups of women down on these trips.

Ron and I talked about the political situation in Haiti. It seems that a group of rebels, mostly old army members, had made their way through the country finally reaching Port-au-Prince. The U.S. tried not to get involved until the rebels were knocking on the gates of the National Palace, and then the U.S. flew Aristide to exile in South Africa. Ron, who is a friend of Aristide's, had been under pressure since Aristide was flown out. There were some jailed Aristide supporters who were broken out by an armed gang. The police accused Ron of helping them, and came to Visitation House armed with machine guns, which they stuck in his face after roughing him up. Ron felt like his time in Haiti might be limited due to the growing anti-Aristide sentiment.

The U.S. had installed an interim Prime Minister, Gérard Latortue, to run the government until elections could be arranged. Security was tenuous. As we drove to Lascahobas, I saw former Haitian Army members wearing their old army uniforms, manning some the roadside police stations. They were wielding ancient looking guns; some of the rifles were duct taped together. In Lascahobas, a group of these rebels were manning the police station and jail across the street from St. Gabriel's Church. They did not give us any trouble, but it was unsettling having them there nonetheless.

Pè Hermann greeted us in the churchyard, and as always it was good to see him. He had been talking to our friend Venel who appeared very thin. He must have lost fifty pounds and was speaking slowly as if tired. "Venel, what's happened to you?" Jean asked. She and Venel have become close friends over the years, corresponding by mail. Venel explained that he had been sick, and was trying to see a doctor. They thought that he might have been developing diabetes.

"I'll be ok." He reassured us speaking in a slow subdued manner. "Can I talk to you later Tom?" He inquired.

"Sure, after we get settled in, I'll meet you back here." I replied.

Later when everyone had moved into their rooms, I met up with Venel and he walked me to his house. It was just a few blocks from St. Gabriel's; we had to duck down a narrow alley walkway to reach his tiny home. Venel and I entered into a small sitting room, and in the back, past the lace-curtain door, were two small bedrooms. He took me on a tour through the house, and out into the back yard where his wife and two young children were playing. It was obvious that his family loved him very much. They had a chadèk tree from which he picked a couple of Haitian grapefruit for us to share while we talked inside.

Venel has had an interesting life. His parents died when he was young, and so another family raised him. While a young man, Venel lived next door to a man who was like a father figure for him, and Venel mentored this man's daughter in return. When this girl came of age, Venel fell in love with her and they married.

Venel directed me into the sitting room while he sliced some chadèk for us to share. I saw Venel's keyboard sitting against the wall. I remembered talking to many of the young men who played in the church band, almost every one of them had told me that Venel had taught them how to play. He is quite a remarkable man.

After serving some chadèk, Venel told me about his work trying to help a group of poor widows in the countryside, and he told me about other projects he was working on, "God has been good to me, and I need to do more to help my people." He pleaded. "Tom. I know you do a lot, but can you help me some with this project?"

We talked for quite a while, and I told Venel that I would like to help everyone in Haiti, but that I just could not. Right now I was trying to complete the school projects, and to make sure that they would continue to run in the future. I told him I really was sorry that I could not do more, but I did give him $20 to help a little.

He was very grateful, "Thank you Tom." He told me with his bright hopeful eyes, and now thinning face. His movements were slow and fatigued, even more so than his usual calm manner. He appeared exhausted from whatever illness he was dealing with, along with his never-ending work to help others. Looking into his eyes and face, I just felt so small, as if all that

I have been doing paled in comparison to his efforts. He seemed to be giving everything he had: his work, his health, and his life. We patted each other's hands, smiled, and then hugged as I left to walk back to the church.

Hermann came out and we caught up on news, everything seemed to be going well. The teachers were asking for another raise since they found out that some of the government teachers were getting raises under Latortue. "We'll talk." I said.

"Tom." Hermann interjected while wearing a mischievous smile, "Your friend Jean Claude is back!"

I smiled and got up quickly, then I called out. "JEAN! RACHEL! Let's go visit a friend."

Walking quickly down the main street, with anticipation, we passed the square and then squeezing through the narrow alleyway to Jean Claude's shaded work yard. I looked around, but did not see anyone. "JEAN CLAUDE!" I yelled, while scanning the yard. The dump truck was partially there, with only the cab and the platform frame, the large metal truck bed was missing. This made me smile, but not as much as when Jean Claude came through the sheet that served as the door to his house.

"Tom!" he exclaimed with a smile. "Tom." He came towards us with his gap-toothed grin, and gravelly laugh. He gave me one of his signature chest crushing hugs, this time lifting me right off the ground.

"Fètatansyon! Jean Claude. Koman ou ye?" "Easy!" I blurted out asking how he was. It was great seeing him; after all of us were introduced, Jean Claude arranged chairs for us to sit in the yard. He was happy to see my daughter Rachel, and called for one of his kids to fetch his oldest son, Claudzi.

Jean Claude told us about his time in jail and his treatment there. He was lucky to have made friends with the jailers, but still the shackles on his legs and wrists had caused permanent damage. He could no longer use his tools or saw for extended periods of time, and he had to stop working. We talked about his wife's death, and he repeated the stories about this and the deaths of his other two wives as well. He called a name, and a woman who was selling cooked food along the curb came into the yard.

"Li neuvo Madanm." Jean Claude said as he introduced his new wife. He had been released from jail shortly after our last visit, and had since remarried. Once Aristide was out of the country, Latortue reviewed the arrest records, and released all political prisoners. His new wife was holding a baby, Jean Claude's eighth child named Ywit Luv, which translates to 'eight love.'

Claudzi arrived, and he told us that he was getting ready to go to Port-au-Prince for secondary school. His dad handed Claudzi a small empty bottle and ordered him off. Claudzi returned a few minutes later with what looked like rum in the bottom of that bottle. "Jean Claude." I said, shaking my head at him as if he were a naughty boy. He only laughed, took a sip, and then put the bottle in his pocket.

Jean Claude showed us his garden, told us about his children, and some more stories about when he was in prison. His personality got him through a rough situation, and he was glad to be back, but it took its toll on him and his family. He was saddened by the loss of his wife, by not being able to work like he used to, and he was drinking more than I remembered. Still, he seemed to be staying responsible to his family from what I could tell. He told us that he would accompany us to Roche-Milat tomorrow; we said that we would see him tomorrow, and then went off.

Hermann was glad to hear the stories, and happy to see us reconnect with our mutual friend. “I like it that you talk to the Haitian people, and that you like people. They like you.” He said. “Also, you always eat any Haitian food we make; some groups come down and don’t eat our food. They seem to be afraid they will get sick. It’s good that you accept our hospitality.”

“It’s not hard to accept.” I said smiling. This seemed obvious, but with so little to give, Haitians only have hospitality, and it is very important that you allow them to give it freely. It makes them equal partners in the relationship. You give, they give, it is important that they participate along with us.

At dinner that night, we all enjoyed that Haitian hospitality. Our relationship with Hermann had grown now to where he would just laugh and laugh when we were together, and he seemed to genuinely enjoy our company. We enjoyed his as well. Hermann told us a story about when the guerilla army came through Lascahobas several months ago. At the time it was getting dark, and everyone in town was afraid of what was going to happen. Word had spread that the guerillas had been robbing and shooting people as they advanced towards Port-au-Prince. That night Hermann decided to drive out around town to make sure everything was all right. As he headed down the main street at night, an armed guerilla jumped out in front of the car pointing a rifle at Hermann; the man was ready to shoot Hermann thinking that he was with the police. Hermann froze in terror at this man ready to shoot him, when suddenly another bystander walking by yelled, “DON’T SHOOT HIM! He’s the priest. Don’t shoot him!” Hermann backed up the car quickly and afterwards stayed home until everything passed.

I could not believe this frightening story told to us while having our usual dinner conversation. Hermann changed the subject, and talked about tomorrow’s plan to visit St. Joseph’s

Chapel in Roche-Milat near the lake. It was just over the ridge from Cabestor; he had received a grant from Europe, and was finishing a new church project there. After dinner everyone went off to get ready for tomorrow's trip, I stayed behind to talk with Hermann.

"Hermann." I asked, obviously concerned. "Why didn't you tell us about your episode with the guerillas sooner?"

"Tom." Hermann replied in Kreyòl, "As a priest, I'm the only person who can look out after my parishioners. Many priests have been killed for speaking up for the people. I never know when I might be killed as well. I just accept this." Then looking at my concern, he just laughed and patted me on the back and we said goodnight.

The next morning we walked the trail towards Cabestor. We passed Phillip's house and he invited us in for a rest, sending his son Tidjo up a tree to get us some coconuts to drink. His wife came out carrying their new son, whose name was Tom. I had never heard of a Haitian named Tom before, and Phillip told me that they named him after me. I was surprised and honored. Later Phillip took me aside and asked me to help him out; he had gotten shot in the leg, and needed some money. I told him what I tell all of the people who ask me for help every time I come to Haiti; I try to help the community and not individuals, because everyone in Haiti needed help. If I help one individual, I would have to help everyone and it would never stop. He was ok with that, but then asked me if he could have my watch, which I gave him. Later Hermann laughed at the story saying, "He undressed you."

Further down the trail, we met up with the mules and climbed up the ridge. The sun shown through the broad green leaves of the banana trees as we passed. Walking along the ridge trail was like walking on the edge of a knife. One step to either side of the trail was a steep drop off, but it was so beautiful. The whole Cabestor valley was stretched out before us; we could see the outlines of the individual gardens, or family farms. I could see the goats and cattle tied up grazing, I could hear singing and men chopping wood. Best of all, I could feel the breeze wash away the heat from the Haitian sun. On the other side of the ridge, I saw Lake Peligre, "Roche-Milat is right on the shore of the lake down there." Jean Claude told us. We then took a side trail that led steeply down from the ridge.

When we arrived at Roche-Milat, I could see St. Joseph's Chapel situated on a landing just above the lake with a stream running behind it. Following the stream down to the lake, we found a beautiful cascading tropical waterfall. The spot where the chapel stood was very picturesque over-looking the lake. We visited with Pelig, Hermann's construction project manager, who was finishing the woodwork around the doors of the chapel. It was good to see Jean Claude help, he was showing the younger carpenters how to saw the plank and smooth it out.

Out in the yard was a small, very temporary school structure made of sticks, a thatched roof, and dried palm leaves attached to the sides for walls. I walked in and introduced myself to the teacher and the students. There were about 25 students ranging from 6 to 18 years of age in this small, one classroom schoolhouse. None of them had books or desks, a few of the older students had a notebook for writing, and yet they all had uniforms. Afterwards while we were sitting out in the yard, we listened to them singing what sounded like the Kreyòl version of "If you're happy and you know it." There is just something right about hearing the sounds of children participating in schoolwork.

We later went swimming in the lake, and afterwards sat on the shore drying. Nearby there were some kids who had built a small fire under a pile of wood, and were making charcoal by smoking it. They were such a raggedy group of little kids. Some of them had shorts without shirts; some had oversized shirts without pants; and some of them had neither A nor B. None of them had shoes; this is the life of these forgotten children of Haiti. When I look at them I could not help but want to do something to help them improve their lives. It is not about giving them stuff; it is about allowing them to live more dignified by helping them help themselves.

Unfortunately we had to leave this relaxing place by the lake to huff our way over the mountain ridge back to Lascahobas. I am in pretty good shape, but with those mountains, and the heat, I don't know how the Haitians can do this every day, especially while carrying those heavy loads.

Back in Lascahobas, we ate dinner, and then afterwards Hermann and I sat on the upper covered walkway balcony to talk before bed. There was a pair of wooden rocking chairs where we could relax together. Things were going well with the transfer of money through Fonkoze to pay the teachers' salaries, and to buy the beans and rice. Last December, Hermann had sent a man to buy the rice in Port-au-Prince, and on the way back the man was beaten to near death, and robbed of the rice. With food prices continuing to rise, this was becoming commonplace.

As we sat relaxing after our hard day of walking, I thought that this would be a good time to give Hermann some good news. I told him that I had finally gotten the money together to build his school on Mon Michel; I thought that he would be pleased to hear this. Instead he told me that he would rather not build up on the mountain, because it would be too hard to carry all of the materials up there.

"Tom." He said. "I'd like you to use that money to build me a school in Roche-Milat."

This was another unexpected request. "Hermann! A third school? I mean, we can build it, but I can't take on any new teachers right now. The trust fund isn't big enough."

Hermann reassured me, "Don't worry about the teachers, I'll work something out with them. But I can get the materials across the lake to build St. Joseph's School in Roche-Milat easier than I can carry them up to Mon Michel. The students are ok in St. Michel's Chapel for now."

"You're hurting me Hermann." I told him.

He just laughed, "Tom, trouble." he said, while continuing to laugh.

As we sat there, I began to think, "I haven't seen Rose Carmel this visit. She always comes around when we're here." Somewhat concerned, I asked, "Where's Rose Carmel?" Bracing for Hermann's reply.

Hermann knew that Rose Carmel and I had a special bond. "Tom." He began, while looking for my response. "She died a few months ago."

I knew that some day she would be gone. She was so frail, but it is always so unexpected. I felt a great loss from her passing, but at the same time I was relieved knowing that she was finally at peace. And I said a little prayer of thanks for Rose Carmel, and for all that she had taught me.

"I'm sorry to hear that." I told Hermann. "I will miss her." We sat rocking together quietly while listening to the night voices from the street below; in time, we said goodnight. As I fell asleep, somehow Lascahobas felt just a bit emptier now that it was missing one of its little souls.

As we prepared to head back to Port-au-Prince the next morning, Venel came by to tell us good-bye. "Here is a letter for you Tom." He told me after we had wished each other well. He is known for leaving letters for people to take back. I put it in my bag, we said our good-byes, and then we all headed back to Port-au-Prince.

After spending the night at Visitation House, we awoke with plans to catch the noon flight home. I asked Ron if I could go visit Anel's family, so he arranged for a quick ride out to their house before our flight left.

Madame Jean was happy to see me, she was not sure if I was going to visit. The children were in the little yard in front of their box-home getting English lessons from a tutor that Anel had arranged for them. Madame Jean showed me some papers she had received regarding their visas, and she asked what they were for. This was great news; we had been waiting for these visa papers to arrive for some time. After I explained to the family what these papers were for, they were beginning to have some hope that they all would finally be reunited. I had the family sign them so that I could carry them back to finish filing their visas. We all kissed on the cheek, and I carried their hugs and kisses back with me for their dad.

Leaving Haiti now, and sitting on our American Airlines flight to Miami, I always liked looking at those Haitians who appeared to be making their first flight to Florida. There was a mixture of anticipation, and anxiety on their faces. I thought of Venel; this might be a good time to take out his letter and see what he had to say. The envelope read:

From: Venel Lamay
To: Tom

As I open it, I notice that there was a twenty-dollar bill placed inside the letter. I read on:

To my friend Tom:

Dear friend. How are you? I think you and your all family are very well, thanks to God. And I am not too bad too, cause of God. I wanted so much to write you to say thank you for the money that you had given to me. I was very happy when I took it from you, but I didn't want to do harm to you because I see all the sacrifices that you do for our community. I didn't want to put you a shame, on the contrary, if I had money I would give some to you, unfortunately, I am poor. I see the love you have in your heart for our poor sisters and brothers. Unfortunately, you do not have enough opportunity for more, now, please, I would like to give it back to you. I always think, when you travel from Virginia to Haiti, you spend a lot, I didn't like to increase your burden. So, I decided to give the money back to you. I pray that God bless you for all sacrifices that you do for us. As a Christian I would like to do like you, but I don't have possibility to do that. I have more than ten widows they have a terrible necessity. I always visit them 3 times a year, but I can't satisfy their needs. I don't know if you could find someone who could help me to take care of them. I do that on my faith, it is Gospel in action. Please don't angry with me for the money return, it because I don't like to increase your difficulty, I know you have enough. You are a man that is unforgettable, others don't understand what happened, but me, by my analysis, I see how you have a great love. I would like to take you as my example. Since 1999 I went school to have more opportunities. Having some contact with foreigners. So I suffer a lot about to see my brothers and sisters suffering like that. What is a problem for me, I see some people has received help, but they never have anything, they still living in the same condition. I would like to change that as Pope J.P. II said. So I ask your help in finding a way of helping the widows and some children too. I just believe in God and my confidence to do this. If you don't want to prove me, you will see the wonderful things that even a president can't realize, that because I believe in God who is the Truth, and who will judge according to the Truth. Dear Mr. Tom, I hope to see you before going or by writing if you don't time.

In Jesus Christ, your brother and friend,

Venel Lamay.
That God bless you, hope to see you.
N.B. excuse me for my mistakes.

What can be said after reading a letter like this? I was stunned. I was in tears holding the returned $20 bill. How far we all have to go, how far away I am from what is expected of me. I thought of how far spiritually I had to go yet before I reached this level of self giving, this level of faith. How far we all were from what is expected of us all; Haiti raises the bar.

Haiti defies a single answer or a single solution. One person, or even a group of people cannot solve the problem that is Haiti. I can work harder and use every skill and talent God has given me, and yet, it is just a drop in the bucket. So many Haitians have given me so many requests, but I have had to learn to block out all of these requests. I have had to block out all of the many needs I have seen around me in Haiti as well. I can only try to accomplish the one thing I have started, and try to finish it the best that I can.

I would like to help Venel and his widows, to help Phillip; I would like to hold all of those orphans in Mother Teresa's Hospital. I would like to do more for Jean Claude, although he never asks me. And I would have liked to do more for Rose Carmel, but now she is at peace. Our culture seems to be all about eliminating suffering, but to live is to suffer. I cannot relieve all of the suffering in Haiti, but I can hold a child, I can comfort a man, and I can visit with a family. I can help with schools that stand as a symbol of hope for a community. They live with their suffering, but they can be strengthened in their journey by the love and hope given by others. In this, although people still suffer, they do not suffer alone. I have taken on some of the suffering of my Haitian friends, and together, in solidarity, we support each other on our mutual journey, which is the human race.

Venel at his home serving chadèk (Haitian grapefruit).

15
Madame Jean

Fanm pou yon tan, manman pou tout tan.

Wife for a time, mother for all time.

I would like to put up a warning here for anyone who is reading this: do not fall in love. If you want to avoid worry and distress, do not let yourself become involved with a group, or with someone else to the point of total surrender in love. That is what happened between me and the people of Haiti. And that is why a twinning project is all about relationship first, because it is from that relationship, that love grows. This love would not allow me to run away, even in hardship. All of the schools, and other projects that have been started so far have happened because of this deep love that I have found myself happily entrapped in. It has been hard to share this love between Haiti and my family, but I have been lucky that my family has been supportive. This has helped me continue to move ahead with each change, and with all the growing pains Haiti would throw at us.

I was contacted by the new pastor at St. Gabriel's in Lascahobas: Pè Raphael Bernadin. He informed me that he was just transferred to this parish by his Bishop. This came as quite of a surprise. I knew that some day we would have another new pastor there, but I really had no warning that Pè Hermann would be changing parishes. My Haitian friend Anel thought that this was an ominous sign; he wondered if something bad had happened to Pè Hermann.

Pè Bernadin assured me that Pè Hermann had just been transferred to a new parish as well, and this explanation sounded reasonable to me. I prepared to meet with Bernadin on my next trip when I asked him via e-mail, "What happened to Pè Hermann?" It was at that point that I found out that Hermann had been moved to his new parish: Sacre Coeur in Cabestor.

"Wow!" I thought. “Sacre Coeur is the chapel where the school is. It's a parish now?”

This put me in a sticky situation since our twin was officially with St. Gabriel's, but the project was located in several of the parish's chapels: Sacre Coeur, St. Michel, and St. Joseph's. Now that Sacre Coeur was a new parish, these chapels would be separated from St. Gabriel’s in Lascahobas. Pè Bernadin was a young pastor, and he was anxious to get started on projects of his own, but I had to tell him that I could not just leave those schools we started orphaned. We would have to talk once I arrived, but I told him that I would probably have to follow the project and transfer our twin relationship to the new parish in Cabestor.

I had not heard from Hermann, and there was no way of reaching him in Cabestor; it was even less accessible than Lascahobas. I had sent the money via Fonkoze for him to get started on St. Joseph's School in Roche-Milat, and we were going to check on the progress of construction when I arrived there in a few months. Once again I was in the dark, and had no way of contacting Hermann. He knew when I was coming down, and I realized from past experiences that I had to just trust that one day the phone would ring, and it would be Hermann calling from someplace to check on the arrangements. He did call about two weeks before I was set to leave. The plan was that Bazilo would meet me with mules along the trail from Lascahobas to Cabestor, and he would get things ready for my stay out in the country. This was going to be a new experience, since there is no electricity, no water, and no roads out there.

With the money for St. Joseph's saved and sent, I had been putting money aside for construction of the long forgotten St. Michel School on Mon Michel. I had only visited there once long ago, and wanted to visit again if possible. Anel and I talked about the changes at the parish, and he assured me that he thought it would work out.

Anel and I continued to work on his family's visa applications; since he did not have birth papers for all of his children, some of them had to take expensive genetic paternity tests. This was done, and we were assured that 'this would be all that was needed.' Well, after all was completed, and we did everything that the immigration department told us we had to do, and more, they just wrote to us saying, "We just cannot process your family's visas at this time." Anel and I were just beside ourselves with frustration. We had done everything they asked of us, we paid every fee. We went and jumped through every hoop they asked us to, even bringing those signed papers back from Haiti. There was no reason given for the 'hold," and they agreed that everything was complete and in order, but that they were just putting their visas on hold anyways.

Time was running out for Anel, especially given that his oldest son was approaching 21 years old. After the age of 21 he would have to apply separately as an adult, and not as a member of the family. Also, the original visa request was only good for one year, and that year would be up in a month. After that the family would have to start all over again. This was unacceptable.

Anel bought a ticket to fly to Haiti, and spent two days in the consulate's office, by then he had his own U.S. citizenship and did not need to make an appointment, which could take nine months. He showed them all of the papers, argued with the people, and finally someone recognized that everything was in order, and that there was not any reason to delay their visas any longer. Of course more money had to be paid, but he was assured that their visas would come in about a month.

When Anel returned, I was overjoyed by this news; he was not. "I won't celebrate until I have the papers in my hand." Anel said. He had been disappointed and burned too many times. He had a similar response when he received his U.S. citizenship, "How can I celebrate while my family is still in Haiti. Tom, I've got to get my family here with me, I just can't take it anymore." Anel told me, almost in tears.

I was getting ready to travel to Haiti in a few months, and the visas did finally arrive. "Anel?" I questioned, "How is your family going to get to the U.S.? They've never flown, they don't know English, and they'll have trouble getting through immigration and customs. It'll be hard for them to get through the airport." We paused for a moment. Then I said, "They're just going to have to come back with me next time."

Anel was overjoyed, "Oh Tom, could you do this for me! I would be so happy." I went ahead and bought tickets for the family, and plans were made for us to travel together to the U.S. on my next trip.

The week before I left, Anel gave me a large pink 'Fairy Princess' suitcase to carry down with me to Haiti. Anel told me. "I have put some new clothes in there for my family, so that they can travel to the U.S. looking good."

This was fine, but I asked Anel, "Did you have to make me carry this silly pink Disney suitcase all the way to Haiti?" We laughed, and he assured me that his wife would meet me at the airport to pick it up when I arrived.

I had made arrangements again for Thimothè to meet me at the airport, and we would travel right to Lascahobas. The newly named Toussaint Louverture Airport in Port-au-Prince had gradually shown improvement since my first visit years ago. Although there was not a mob outside, there still was a large, though more orderly crowd waiting for people. In the crowd I spotted Madame Jean, it was great seeing her with her big smile. I happily gave her possession of the pink princess suitcase, and we agreed to have the family meet next week at Visitation House. I warned her that it had changed its name to Matthew 25 House, but that it was in the same location. We hugged, and then I met Thimothè for our trip up Mon Kabrit.

On the way I talked with Thimothè about whether he had heard from Ron Voss since Ron had to leave. Ron had been out of Haiti for just short of a year. With all of the trouble Ron found himself in after Aristide went into exile, he had to give up Visitation House, and temporarily leave behind his other projects. Visitation House was now being run by The Haiti Parish Twinning Program coordinated by Theresa Patterson out of Nashville Tennessee. They had taken over running the guesthouse, and were now calling it Matthew 25 House. I felt that the house just would not be the same without Ron there.

Haiti had held its elections, and their new president was Renè Prèval. He has been working on building up Haiti's infrastructure, and we could see the fruits of this work along our trip up Mon Kabrit. There was a massive road construction project underway leading from Croix des Bouquets to Mirebalais. I have seen construction like this started before, but they never finished the road, only to have the work washed away. We will see if Prèval can finally get this road paved.

At St. Gabriel's Parish in Lascahobas, I was greeted by Pè Bernadin. He is a large man in height and girth, and very polished in his presentation. He was happy to see me, and he had prepared a welcome lunch. Looking around the churchyard, I could see that he was busy fixing the walks and gardens. There were different women working in the parish kitchen, Justine and Chantal had gone to help Hermann in his new parish.

Thimothè, Bernadin, the associate priest, and myself sat down to lunch, and we talked about how we would work the new relationship. I once again had to delicately apologize for the uncomfortable position I was put in, but I could not leave the schools in the Cabestor Valley orphaned. I had to move our twin relation to the new Sacre Coeur Parish from St. Gabriel's. After a while he understood what I was saying, and he understood that I was not backing away from St. Gabriel's because he was the new pastor. I had changed pastors before when Pè Pol left. I did promise him that I would make it my responsibility to find him a new twinned parish in Virginia. We also talked about how he might want to approach this new relationship, since I had been through it before. I spent the night in the parish, and I was told that Bazilo would meet me in the morning with the mules.

Through the night it rained hard. I met Bazilo, but the river was too high for us to cross immediately. I spent the morning visiting with Jean Claude, and he seemed to be doing well. He still was not working full time, but he was able to help out occasionally on small jobs. His children were playing in the upside-down cab shell, which was all that was left of the once mighty Mack truck. They were all growing so fast. I said good-bye, and finally left once Bazilo called us to go.

The water was starting to go down, so we decided to try and cross the river. With us attempting to cross this high river water, we created another one of those dramatic scenes for all the local spectators. In Haiti everything is a small drama, but especially when people get to watch the blan try and cross the high, fast moving river, on a mule. I think they were taking bets as to whether I would make it or not. The odds were not looking good for me, but I did make it.

Even with the rain last night, the day was looking nice and sunny. I walked some, and rode the mule some, along with a few young Haitian men and Bazilo. As I traveled down the trail towards Cabestor, I once again had that feeling of belonging as I returned to my spiritual classroom: Haiti. Each time I return, I am amazed at what can be discovered when I reach out into the unknown world of poverty's richness. I started out walking, and I like this; it gets me closer to the land, and the people of Haiti. I get to speak and walk in solidarity with my brothers and sisters, I get to feel the heat, hear the sounds, and smell the country. I have found that I look over this great land of Haiti and at its people with love, but still through my western eyes. How my heart was about to be opened, along with my eyes this day.

After a while, I took my turn riding the mule, this was a luxury and I was glad to accept the hospitality. Up on my animal, I could take even more time to look over the hills, green with sunshine, and the fields, rich with labor and life. So on I went, getting closer to our visit with the waiting schoolyard full of singing Haitian children and their teachers welcoming us as they have in the past. The wet trail was a bit difficult to maneuver on the mule, and in some ways it would have been easier to continue walking on stable ground. I became separated from the Haitians who had walked ahead, and my animal was getting stuck sinking into the mud. Finally the mule walked up onto a narrow trail, a strip of higher ground that followed up next to the muddy road. I could see trouble ahead, and sure enough, when the high ground ran out the mule tried to jump back down onto the muddy road: CRASH! I was thrown off his back and somehow survived the fall finding myself on my knees in the deep mud with my hands buried past my wrists, and my face and glasses splattered with mud. I was so close, only a quarter mile from the school, what am I going to do with all this mud on me?

A Haitian women saw me fall and asked if I was ok, I told her yes but that I could use some water. So this stranger on the road ran to fetch me a pan with a pitcher of water and took me into her yard to care for me. What proceeded was one of the most beautiful acts of loving kindness I have experienced. She took my hands into hers and kindly, and gently poured the pitcher of water over them while lovingly rubbing and massaging the mud from my hands. As she worked the dirt from my hands, I could not help but see Jesus washing the feet of his disciples. She then took a clean cotton dress of hers from inside her house to dry my hands and wipe the mud from my face. I was so thankful for this kindness not only freely given to a stranger, but also given in such a loving and gentle way. I thanked her in Kreyòl and gave her a hug and a blessing before reluctantly remounting my beast. As I rode into the schoolyard Father Hermann greeted me looking concerned, "I heard you fell! Are you alright?"

"Yes." I said, but he had no idea just how well I was. I will keep this memory with me always, but I share this story with you now as freely as it was given to me then.

After Hermann saw that I was ok, he welcomed me to his new parish. It is always good to get back to Cabestor and see the students and teachers. Sonrius, the school's director, was not there because his mother had died, and he was far away with his family. We talked about what it was like for Hermann to be stationed out here in the country without easy access to roads, phone or electric. It was difficult, but Hermann told me that he actually petitioned the Bishop to be moved out here. He saw the needs of the people; and now with the new schools, this community was growing. Bishop Kebreau gave Hermann special permission to try and make a go of it in Cabestor over the next three years. I was surprised that Hermann asked to be stationed out here in the country, he seemed like such a 'city boy' when we first met, but he had changed. I could tell that he really enjoyed being out here in the country, close to the

Haitian people. "They really need me to be here." He told me. He seemed relaxed, comfortable, as if he belonged here. Living out in Cabestor was more like camping, but Justine and Chantal made sure I was comfortable. Tomorrow, we would climb over the ridge to meet up with Pelig whose work was progressing well with the construction of the new school in Roche-Milat.

The next morning we left Cabestor traveling to Roche-Milat. Cabestor is in a valley with a tall mountain ridge to the north, where Mon Michel is located, and then the shorter mountain ridge to the south, over which Roche-Milat is located besides the shore of Lake Peligre. We climbed and then walked along this mountain ridge, with a view that was even more beautiful than I had remembered. It was the rainy season, so everything was green. Looking back into the valley, I could see the small compound, which is Sacre Coeur Parish; it looked so small and almost hidden amongst the lush trees and gardens of the valley. Looking towards Lascahobas, I could see a majestic range of mountains that was encircled by a mist of clouds from the evening's sprinkling. Large leaves from banana trees and palm trees filled the valley below. The farms formed a patchwork of fields dotted by small houses up and down the valley floor. Lake Peligre was 'full pond' as we descended towards Roche-Milat. When we came over the final hill, I could see the foundation of the new St. Joseph's school rising from above the side of the lake. It was a beautiful setting; the school sitting high up off the water, surrounded by the trees, blue sky, and the lake water. Once again I had that sense of wonder and pride at the birth of another new child: this new school.

We met up with Pelig who was wearing this bright red hat, it looked like one I had seen Haitian women wearing, but it kept the sun off his head. "Tom!" Pelig greeted me. "Konman ou ye?"

We embraced, and caught up on things before resting with some water. Pelig was still looking taught, strong, and wiry;

and he continued to have an energy, and a humor about him as he proudly pointed out the work they had accomplished so far. He showed me around the construction site of the 'L' shaped, five-room schoolhouse. It stood so proudly up on that ridge overlooking the lake. I thought to myself, "This would be a $5 million property in the U.S." But it's Haiti, and there were no other structures even close to this quality along the lake's shoreline.

Remember, there are no roads out here; everything was brought in by the same type of dugout canoe that I first rode with Pè Pol. Everything was carried in by these canoes: sand, rocks, block, steel rebar, cement and wood. All dropped off along Highway #3, carried to the shore, and then canoed to this site, little by little, using volunteers from the community. As we sat there talking, I could see people taking turns carrying buckets of sand up from the shore. Men were carrying cinder blocks to the site one-by-one. After a few trips, people would sit and talk, and then go on their way. I could not imagine how much people power it took to build this, and they were more than half way done.

One of the construction workers was less than thrilled to see a blan watching them work, and starting singing a Kreyòl song about 'the blan' to his fellow workers. When I responded to his song in Kreyòl, "I like the song you're singing about me." He seemed surprised, and later told Hermann, "The white guy knows Kreyòl." After that he showed me around, and we were good friends joking and getting to know each other. Finally it was time to get back before dark. I enjoyed the 'ridge ride' as the sun was setting, and once again felt so at peace in my home away from home: Haiti.

That evening, as we ate by lantern light, Hermann said that he had arranged for Sayel (Sigh-yeal) to escort me on a climb up the mountain to visit St. Michel. Sayel is one of the local men who served as the Deacon at Sacre Coeur while it was a chapel.

Hiking up Mon Michel on the trail from Cabestor was the hike that Sister Laurette had said, "Would kill you." Hermann thought I could make it. Along the way, he wanted Sayel to point out two mountain springs that were good sources of fresh drinking water. Although it was the rainy season now, once dry season comes, all of the springs down in the valley dry up and there is no reliable drinking water. We had built a well house during construction of Sacre Coeur School, but the well had long since dried up, and was now housing the generator. Hermann had always provided bottled water for my visits, but out here in Cabestor Bazilo had to carry them in by mule.

Lack of clean drinking water is a major health problem around the world, and obviously for Haiti as well. The World Health Organization estimates that 1.1 billion people die each year from lack of clean water. Diseases such as hepatitis, dysentery, malaria, cholera, typhoid, and parasites, all can be traced to a lack of clean water. Fatal diarrhea is the second most common cause of death among children. Also, simple soap and water cleaning can prevent many skin infections. Deaths due to diarrheal illnesses can be cut in half, just by providing clean drinking water. Two of Jean Claude's wives died from diseases caused by a lack of clean water.

Given this, Hermann had the idea of capturing this spring water by building cisterns and piping the water down to the village. This sounded like a great idea, and I was excited to check out the springs on my way up the mountain.

The next morning, Sayel, Bazilo, and I prepared for our trek. Hermann made sure we were loaded with carbs before we left: plantain, rice, and manyok root. He also gave me some cut up sugar cane for along the way. We walked fairly fast up rolling hills past small farm-huts and gardens, resting occasionally to look down at the view. We passed the two springs about a mile into our walk, both were flowing nicely, but especially the high spring, which formed a pool next to the outflow. Children were filling their jugs with water, and ran as soon as I approached. They were so frightened by seeing me that they dumped their water out and took off running down the trail screaming. These springs were a great source of clean water given the fact that they were coming right out of the side of the mountain, but as soon as the water started flowing down the streambed, it became contaminated by people and animals. This was going to be a big project trying to get this water down the valley; I would have to talk with Hermann about how we were going to do this.

We continued to walk, up and up, then higher and higher, over one ridge, and then another. It was a good climb, but it became ridiculous once we reached the final ascent. The view of the valley and lake Pelilgre was wonderful, and we could see over the ridge we had climbed to get to Roche-Milat. Even as steep as the last kilometer was, we were still walking through someone's field of Pitimil or millet. I could not believe someone was farming way up here. The sugar cane Hermann gave me came in handy, my legs were burning trying to climb up, and my heart was pounding. We passed a stream of cool water and scooped it over our heads, "God's air conditioner." Bazilo said in Kreyòl while smiling. I had to agree.

Finally I could hear the children, as we reached the top of Mon Michel. There was a small rectory on a rocky landing overlooking the churchyard below. I could hear the children singing and working on lessons in the makeshift chapel/school. It was worth the climb just to hear the life in one of our schools that I had not seen in such a long time, but had thought about so often. We took a few minutes to dry off, and rest before making our surprise visit to St. Michel School. We all stood at the edge of the summit looking over that awe-inspiring view of Lake Peligre, the mountains, and the entire Central Plateau of Haiti. It all looked so peaceful and quiet from up here.

When we finally made our entrance at the school, the teachers were quite surprised to see us, but they did remember me from our visit years ago. We caught up on how the students were doing, and they made me talk to each of the classes in Kreyòl, and say hello. The students were intrigued by the strange white visitor, but they had all heard of "Tom," and they figured that I must be him. They all had that same look of wanting in their eyes; young and old, they seemed so honestly grateful to be in school and to be learning. This is why I go to Haiti, to be recharged with their looks of appreciation, which makes all the work worthwhile. The classes were let out on recess while the teachers and I talked. The school was now up to 360 students in eight classes, and they had hired a fifth teacher for the older classes. I wanted to take some pictures, so the teachers told me to wait a minute while they directed the students into an assembly.

Outside in the yard the students lined up into eight rows in front of the Haitian flag. They looked like a xylophone set up from smallest to tallest. After singing me one of their songs I congratulated them for all of the hard work they were doing to help their country, just by studying and going to school. I also asked them if they would like a nice new school; to which they all screamed a resounding "Wi!"

"How about a school like the one in Cabestor? Would you like that up here?" I asked enthusiastically.

"Wi!" They repeated, with the teachers almost as excited as the children.

"Well, you are going to get one once we can bring the material up here." I told them in Kreyòl, to which they all clapped and smiled. As they reentered the chapel to restart classes, I stood by the steps touching each one of their heads or arms as they passed. I cannot describe the emotion I felt, but it was love. Looking into each one of them, I had the same feeling that runs through you just before you are ready to cry for someone you love. Afterwards I just had to sigh, and stand there awhile. The teachers showed me the spot were the school would be built. Finally, we said good-bye, and walked down. After working so hard to get up here, I had not thought about having to go back, and although it was mostly downhill, I was ready to call a cab.

When we finally arrived back in Cabestor, Hermann was amazed that I had made it up and back. He was really tickled by this, laughing and hurrying around to get me a Prestige and some food. Hermann always enjoyed it when I would experience something Haitian. I enjoyed seeing him happy.

I was really worn out that evening. After a rest and a bucket shower in the makeshift shed, Hermann and I got together in the small rectory for a late dinner. It was dark by then, and a hard rain started to fall as the evening went on. I talked with Hermann about the water project; we both agreed that it was a great idea, and that it was badly needed. I could see that in order to make this clean water project happen, and happen well, it was going to take a lot more technical expertise than just Hermann, Pelig, and myself could design. I had seen other projects in Haiti that were poorly planned, and I told Hermann not to start working on this until I could find some engineering advice back in the States first. Resources are too scarce, and this project was too important to botch it up.

We talked about my visit to St. Michel, and he enjoyed the stories. I told him that now we could finally build the school up there, I had saved enough money to get started after the rainy season ended next year. He again was happy for this, but asked if he could use some of the money to build a new kitchen and a store here in Cabestor. The old kitchen was falling down, and he had an idea for a small store to sell school uniforms and textbooks to the kids. They had to buy them anyways, but this way the profit could be used to help pay for much needed teaching supplies, and we could provide textbooks for the poorer students.

"Hermann, you're trouble." I said to his laughter, but we agreed to start on those projects while I saved more for the eventual building of St. Michel School. "How many times have we tried to build this school?" I thought.

We sat for a while under the porch overhang watching the rains come down. To our surprise, a figure appeared through the darkness and the rain. As the person was walking towards us I realized that it was Sonrius! I could not believe this, "Bonswa Sonrius." I greeted him, even in his soaked state. "It's great to see you. What are you doing here? I heard that your mother had died, and I'm sorry about that."

"Good to see you Tom." Sonrius said, "Yes, I was with my family over the mountain, but I knew you were here and wanted to make sure I saw you before you left."

Hermann and I sat and talked with Sonrius for about an hour. I was amazed to see that he had walked such a long distance, over the mountains, and in the dark while it was raining, just to say hello. He was carrying his dress shoes, and had on a dress shirt and dress pants that were rolled up to his knees so that they would not get muddy. He was trying to make a good impression, and he did more than that. All was well with the students, they were working hard, but it is difficult teaching them when their parents do not have a history of being educated; they cannot help them with homework.

Finally he had to leave, "Sonrius, you're not going to walk back in the rain and dark are you?" I inquired.

"Yes Tom, I grew up around these mountains, I know my way back." He reassured me.

I gave him a firm embrace, and told him how impressed I was that he would take the trouble to come all this way to see me, especially with his mother's death. "You didn't have to do this Sonrius, thank you." With that we said good-bye and he walked off into the rain and darkness, barefoot, with his pants rolled up to his knees, and carrying his shoes.

"Hermann, that's amazing." I said. Herman just laughed at my amazement as he usually does, and then I continued to listen to Hermann tell me all about his dreams for the people of this valley.

Hermann accompanied me back to Port-au-Prince, this time on a real bus. When we passed through Mirebalais, I saw the Rotary International sign greeting visitors to town. I asked Hermann if he knew of any Rotarians in Mirebalais, since he used to be the pastor there. He did; and I told him to find me a Rotary contact so that I could get a grant to help fund the water project. He said he would work on that.

We arrived at Matthew 25 House, formerly Visitation House; and Sister Mary, the host, greeted us. Hermann was staying with his sister in town; we agreed to meet again for the dedication of St. Joseph's school in about six months. With this Hermann was off.

After getting settled in, I asked Sr. Mary how things were going with her new guesthouse. It definitely looked like she and Theresa Patterson had spruced it up, giving it more of a 'woman's touch.' Although the house was still in transition, all was going well. Ron was lying low in the U.S., and would probably not be hosting Visitation House any longer. I told Sister that I was expecting Madame Jean and the family to spend the night with us before our adventure tomorrow as we traveled to, 'Lot bo dlo.' the other side of the ocean: Miami.

Riding the ridge to Roche-Milat.

Boys making charcoal at Roche-Milat, on Lake Peligre.

Sayel on the route up Mon Michel. Lake Peligre below.

Teachers and students of St. Michel's School: Mon Michel.

16
The Last Waltz

Ou wè sa ou genyen, ou pa konn sa ou rete.

You see what you've got, but you don't know what is coming.

Sister Mary and I spent the evening catching up on news. There was a group coming to stay at Matthew 25 House the next morning, but for now I was her only guest. I was getting concerned because Madame Jean and the family had not yet shown up; it was getting dark and beginning to rain. Finally the guard at the gate told us that visitors had arrived, and there she was with her four children. All of them dressed in the new clothes that Anel had sent for them. Sister offered them some late food and I sat with them while they ate. I was excited about their first airplane flight, and the fact that finally, after all this work and all this time, the family would be reunited. I had dreamed of this day when they would get to leave Haiti, and I often wondered what it would be like; now it was about to really happen.

For some reason the family was not as excited as I was. I think that they were having some mixed feelings. Although they were heading towards a new, but unknown future, they were also leaving friends and family here in Haiti, a place that has been home no matter what the condition. It was a quiet evening. Then Madame Jean and the family went off to bed: their last night in Haiti.

The next morning we made it through the Toussaint Louverture Airport without any problems, and all of the children seemed to enjoy the acceleration of take-off. We landed in Ft. Lauderdale, and since they needed temporary visas, we had to go to the end of the immigration line. We had three-and-a-half hours to make our connection, but I certainly wanted to get through all of this as quick as possible. When we finally made it to the immigration counter, I spoke for the family.

The immigrations agent inquired about my schools in Haiti asking, "Do you teach them English in your schools? Why don't these people learn English, or an international language?"

"They can speak French." I responded.

The agent replied. "That's not an international language."

I was stunned by this response from an official U.S. Immigration agent, and corrected the man. The agent was finishing up with us, and we found out that we had to go to the office and have their temporary visas made. It took another hour for this, and when we finally finished, we had only 45 minutes to go through customs, walk to another terminal, check in, pass through security, and get to our gate. We were slowed down by mom's high heels, the children's fear of escalators (they had never seen one before), and all the usual airport lines. But we did make it just as the plane was boarding. I was just a little bit frazzled after all of this; thank heavens for the in-flight drink service.

We had planned to meet Anel and my friend Jean who had volunteered to drive them home from the airport in her van. As we approached the security exit, and the family saw their father, they immediately started running. It was a mob scene, and the people looking on had no idea what was happening. But I believe that in this one moment, during that five-minute group hug, six years of emotions from separation were let out. There were so many tears, so much holding on; it was as if after finally getting their family together, they were not going to let each other go. They hugged and cried, and then hugged again.

Finally Jean loaded up the van and headed home with all of them. Even with the big van, there was little room for all of them to sit with all of their bags. They were squeezed in together, but it was much like their tap-tap's back home: no big deal. At one point Anel started singing one of the songs that they all knew from church, and when he started singing, the whole family joined in the song. It was a happy, joyous reunion. It was the best of times.

After Anel and the family were situated in their apartment, and started getting used to their new home, I began thinking about this clean water project. I asked around for help from some engineering firms, or friends who were engineers, but I did not get anywhere. Finally I was introduced to an engineer at Virginia Tech by the name of Theo Dillaha. He was with a group called "Engineers without Borders." This group was fashioned after Doctors without Borders, but obviously their focus was to help with engineering projects in developing countries. He was very busy, but agreed to help design a plan for this project. "You need to go back with a G.P.S. machine and get me some data on the location of these springs." He told me.

I had organized a men's group to visit Haiti in a few months for the St. Joseph's School dedication. Three of the men were engineers, and one of them had a G.P.S. machine to take with us. The other member was Tommy Denton, husband of Jean. He had been with me on several past trips. It was nice traveling with 'the guys,' especially since the accommodations at the new rural parish were more rustic.

Everyone enjoyed the visit, and one day Sayel took us on a tour of 'the zone.' That is the word for the rural neighborhood. Sayel took us way up top one of the mountains to his home; it was nice visiting his family, but it was strenuous. After that hike I figured the group was ready to travel to St. Joseph's for the school dedication in the morning.

The next day we took our turns on the mules or walking over the ridge on the way to Roche-Milat. I actually preferred being on my own feet. The view from the ridge was as beautiful as ever. We made our descent towards the chapel; walking through the lush overgrowth of trees, and banana groves gave the trip a jungle feeling. Finally we climbed over the rise and saw the new school with all the people waiting, I knew that we were almost home. The scene was much the same as when we had visited Mon Michel that first time. The yard was crowded with visitors, girls ready to dance, and the school was decorated for the fèt-la. The work that Pelig's men had done on the school was outstanding, the school looked even better than Sacre Coeur. Pelig was there, and I congratulated him on a job well done.

Hermann motioned that it was time to begin the ceremony, so we entered the church. The ceremony proceeded as before, with the drumming, the choir and dancing; this time some of the school kids put on skits for us. Hermann had asked me to say something to the people in Kreyòl, and this is what I told them:

Good afternoon everyone, we are so happy to be here to celebrate the opening of your new school. Do you all know what the lambi is? Every Haitian knows the lambi don't they? Well I'm going to tell you a Haitian proverb:

Depi Lambi konen, tout moun konnen
Sak pral genyen.
Se nouvel Ayisyan.
Nouvel ki soti byen lwen.

Translated: When the lambi sounds then everyone will know what's going to happen. It's Haitian news, good news that comes from far away.

[I made a gesture as if blowing a lambi.] Well I'm sounding the lambi for all of you today, because I'm bringing you good news. The good news that I'm bringing you is that God has not forgotten you. Even out here far away from everything, God has not forgotten you. God has heard all of your prayers for help.

Now you may ask me, "Tom, how do we know God has not forgotten us? We can't see God. We cannot hear God. He doesn't speak to us. So how do we know?"

Well, I have another Haitian proverb for you:

Nèg pale san fè, men Bondye fè san pale.

People talk but don't do anything, God does things but doesn't talk. Do you see that school out there? God built that school for you, and every time you pass that school I want you to remember that God has not forgotten you. God will never forget you.

I then started them singing one of their favorite songs, to which everyone loudly sang and clapped.

"Se pou ou chante. Se pou ou danse. Se pou ou rele. Viv Bondye Gramet-la." (It's for you we sing, we dance, we say: long live God, the great Master.)

After this we all went out following Hermann who walked us past the school, blessing it with water while the choir and people sang along. After this the festival began with talking, story telling, laughing, food, and of course: gwog (fruit flavored kleren).

The next day in Cabestor we all recounted stories of people we had met, and for those men for whom this was their first Haitian experience, they just could not say enough about what they had seen.

Later that day we took the G.P.S. machine from Cabestor to the two mountain springs and made satellite guided measurements of their locations, and elevations to be analyzed back in Virginia. It was amazing to me that this little hand held machine would allow us to make measurements of these springs which were out here in rural Haiti by connecting to satellites up in orbit. But it did.

On the way to Port-au-Prince, I asked Hermann to stop in Mirebalais so that he could introduce me to his friend who was the president of the Mirebalais Rotary Club: Francklin Joseph. Francklin and I agreed to work in concert for this water project. His involvement was key to obtaining grant money through Rotary International, and luckily for us, Rotary was pushing international clean water projects that year.

During the flight home, I had to reflect on where the project has come from those first days with Pè Pol. Now we had two schools constructed, a third finally planned and ready to go, the kitchen and store underway, and in a few years a clean water project. During this last trip the teachers told me that they were going to build a little home for me near Sacre Coeur so that I could stay there. I told them I would like that, after which they clapped and whooped. I still do not know why, but out in this rural valley of Haiti, I feel more at home than I do at home.

Back in Salem, I sent the G.P.S. measurements to Theo Dillaha at Virginia Tech. He had a team of students and fellow faculty members who were coming up with a plan to construct cisterns to capture, and then pipe the water to a system of cisterns on the way down to its central location in Cabestor. I presented this plan to the Rotary Club of Salem, and they had taken on this water project as their primary international project for the year. They would help to raise the money for construction, and allow us to apply for matching grants.

Hermann had been working with Pelig to finish construction of the kitchen and bookstore in Cabestor now that St. Joseph's School had been completed. I had sent the money down so that the local people from Mon Michel could start carrying building supplies up the mountain before the summer rains started. The rest of the money would be sent in November once the hurricane season ended. It looked like we would be keeping Hermann and Pelig busy for a while.

Anel and his family were becoming accustomed to the U.S.; the children were in school and learning English well. The older son was working and going to community college, but was in the process of joining the U.S. Air Force to further his education and training. Only the mom was having trouble with her English, and although while in Haiti she had a school where she taught cake baking and decorating, she could not find a similar job here due to her poor English skills. She ended up working as a housekeeper for a local hospital. Everyone was happy to be together, but they still missed their home in Haiti.

I have three daughters, and my youngest, Michelle, had not yet visited Haiti; it was time. We had planned a trip for Easter week, and I went down with Jean, Michelle and my wife Leah. The trip went well, and we had a surprise discovery in Lascahobas; the parish was having their big feast day celebration during our stay. I had heard of this festival before, but had never been down in Lascahobas for it. The big day started with a huge Mass, attended by all the priests in the Diocese, and many visiting dignitaries. The church was packed to overflow capacity; it was a wonderful celebration.

The best part was afterwards, when everyone stayed for the big party in and around the churchyard. I had a chance to touch base with all of the prior assistant priests I had met over the years: Pè Wilcoxson, Pè Wadler, Pè Bertrand, and Pè Jethro who was now the interim Bishop while they were searching for a permanent Bishop. I also ran into my old friend Pè Pol. It was nice to see him; we talked about his new parish out in the country, he has a similar arrangement to Pè Hermann's. We quickly caught up on old times, and then he left on his motorcycle. His parting words to me were, "I am dancing wherever I may be." And with a deep throaty laugh he was off. It is always good to see Pol. That day was a day to reflect on all of the people I had met through the years working in Haiti.

Michelle had a chance to meet Jean Claude and Claudzi. Claudzi was visiting from school in Port-au-Prince; he was home to visit during the parish festival. Claudzi had certainly grown into a responsible young man. Jean Claude had not changed, and we spent the afternoon with him and his children out in the yard, under the shady tree.

Back in Cabestor we met up with Pelig who was working on the construction of the new kitchen. Hermann was getting everything ready for the Easter Celebration the next day. Michelle was fitting right in, and was enjoying her first trip to Haiti. Being a young American, she was an instant hit with the kids. During dinner I joked with Hermann telling him that Michelle is a dancer, and maybe we could put some bananas on her head so that she could dance along with the other kids. He laughed and said, "Whatever you want Tom, I will do for you."

Later that night before bed we had another special treat, the skies were clear, dark, and filled with stars. There were more stars than I had ever seen in the States. Remember that there are no lights anywhere near Cabestor. The sky was thick with stars. I did not know that the sky could be like this; we just stood in the yard, our eyes gapping at the wonder of it all.

A Haitian youth saw us, and asked Michelle, "What are you looking at?"

She told him, "The stars."

Perplexed he asked, "Don't you have stars in America?"

"Yes we have stars," Michelle said still looking up, "But not like this!"

Easter morning came, and both the church and the yard were filled with people; they had walked in from all around the zone. It was a similar scene to when we dedicated Sacre Coeur School years ago. The ceremony proceeded as I had experienced them in the past, and Michelle was amazed by the spirit of it all. When it came time to bring up the gifts, and the dancers were getting ready in the back with bananas, chickens, fruit and other produce, Hermann gave me and Michelle a nod as if to say, "You can join them if you'd like."

"Michelle." I directed, "Kick off your shoes and go back there and join the dancers."

Before Michelle knew what she was doing, we had her shoes off, and she was walking barefooted in her skirt down the center aisle from our seats up front. As soon as Michelle stood and started walking towards the back, the congregation sat up in surprise. You could hear everyone talking and watching and wondering what the blan was doing.

Once the dancers started coming in from the back, and then Michelle joined them, the chatter became even louder and more vigilant. Amazement could be seen on people's faces as Michelle learned to mimic the barefoot dance steps, and then she came dancing down the aisle with the procession of other girls. Michelle had noticed that the girl in front of her had a chicken on her head; she thought it was dead until it opened its eyes and started blinking at her.

"Oh my gosh! She has a live chicken on her head!" Michelle exclaimed to herself, still not missing a dance step.

All of the girls looked so beautiful coming down the aisle, but it was so much more special with the one blan, the white girl, joining the parade. All of these girls were offering not only the fruits and animals that they were carrying, but they were also offering the gift of their dance. This time, Michelle had become part of the offering with her dance as well: her arms and dress swinging in unison with her Haitian sisters. The whole scene was an icon, symbolic of the unity, and the solidarity that had grown between our two communities. It was a very powerful moment, and I could sense that everyone there recognized it.

Hermann was ecstatic, and afterwards he told the congregation, "Did you see that! The blan danced with us. That shows that we are all unified in the church." It was a special, special moment. One I will never forget.

I guess that the O.L.P.H. Haiti Project has also been a long dance between our two communities. At times we have had some missteps, but we have also shared some beautiful waltzes.

Out in the yard that afternoon the children continued to play with Michelle, and teach her some of their games, as she taught them some of hers. We talked with folks, joked with people, and watched families and friends spending time together. This courtship that had begun with a letter, has continued through this dance of visits and shared struggles, and has still not ended. The child that was born through the shared love of our two communities has grown to adolescence. I was not going to leave this child orphaned, so the relationship has to continue. It still needs to grow. I could never have imagined that we would be where we are today, and only time will tell where this love will take us in the future. I suspect the unexpected, and I suspect that it will be wonderful!

Michelle dances with the children of Cabestor.

Cabestor Valley homesteads and gardens.

St. Joseph's School.

Students: St. Joseph's, Roche-Milat

Fresh water, mountain spring on the trail up Mon Michel.
This will supply the future cistern
and clean water project for
the Cabestor Valley.

The End.

Group Discussion Questions

1) Have you had a personal experience of poverty, or with poverty? If so, describe it. Did it make you want to move towards action, or retreat into avoidance?

2) If you or your group is considering work in Haiti, write down what your expectations are. What do you hope to accomplish? What do you think you will discover? Seriously ask yourself, "WHY am I going to Haiti at this time in my life?" Be honest.

3) If you have returned from a trip to Haiti, how has the experience changed you? Describe the experience as if you were writing to a close friend.

4) What do you think it means to 'be in solidarity' with the people of Haiti? Was the author in solidarity? How? List some of the ways.

5) In this book, what do you think was 'The Lambi's Call' for the author? What was it that motivated him to continue working for the people of Haiti? How was this motivation acquired?

6) In The Lambi's Call, the author tells many stories about several people. Which of these stories or characters spoke strongly to you, and why?

7) Prior to reading The Lambi's Call, what images came to mind when you heard of Haiti? After reading this book, have these images changed? Elaborate?

8) Dr. Fame put down his 'medical bag' when he started working on forming a relationship with the people of Haiti. He talks about "Being rather than doing." What are the pros and cons of the 'Medical Mission' model, versus the 'Twinning Relationship' model of working in Haiti?

9) If after spending some time with the people in your Haitian community, and after forming a good working relationship with this community you have mutually decided on a project: do you have a plan to provide for the long-term sustainability of this project? Describe it.

About O.L.P.H. Haiti Project

O.L.P.H. Haiti Project
314 Turner Rd.
Salem, VA 24153
540-387-0491
http://Haiti.OLPHSalem.org
fame5@verizon.net

Proceeds from the sale of this book help provide salaries for the Haitian teachers through the O.L.P.H. Haiti Trust.

The O.L.P.H. Haiti Project gladly accepts tax-deductible donations to help pay for the student lunch program as well.

Larger gifts are also gladly accepted, and will be invested through the O.L.P.H. Haiti Trust. The income produced helps to expand the number of teachers we can hire at these schools.

If you would like to consider gifts of cash, stock transfers, life insurance, or other bequests, please contact Tom Fame above, or through the publisher (see back of book).

Organization Contact Information

Diocese of Richmond Haiti Twinning Program
Patrice Schwermer
Haiti Outreach, Diocese of Richmond
7800 Carousel Lane
Richmond, VA 23294-4201
804-622-5129
pschwermer@richmonddiocese.org
http://www.richmonddiocese.org/haiti

Partners In Health
641 Huntington Ave, 1st Floor
Boston, Massachusetts 02115
USA
Phone: 617-432-5256
Fax: 617-432-5300
info@pih.org
http://www.pih.org

The Parish Twinning Program of the Americas
Theresa Patterson
208 Leake Avenue
Nashville, TN 37205 U.S.A.
Parishprogram@aol.com
http://www.parishprogram.org

"What we strive for in a twinning relationship, Tom has carried to perfection. His love story with the people of Haiti is warm, tender and genuinely heartfelt. As Tom has so beautifully illustrated, the ultimate gift of twinning is that when we labor alongside those who suffer and are poor, we bring about our own mutual liberation."

Theresa Patterson, P.T.P. of the Americas

"If you are unable to visit Haiti yourself, read this book and experience the gift that the Haitian people have given to so many of us -- the gift of love that teaches us "just how far we have to go spiritually." If you are preparing to visit Haiti, let Tom help you understand how remarkable it is to be able to encourage someone "just by being present to them." If you know Haiti well, let his deep insights illuminate your own experience. His storytelling is sure to leave you full of joy."

Anne Hastings, Director of Fonkoze

Fonkoze U.S.A.
John Mercier, Director
50 F Street, NW, Suite 810
Washington, DC 20001
Phone: 202-628-9033
Fax: 202-628-9035
jmercier@fonkoze.org
http://www.fonkoze.org

Matthew 25 House
Delmas 33, #6 Rue A. Martial
Port-au Prince, Haiti
Phone: 011-509-511-7273
Cell: 011-509-493-1900
matthew25house@yahoo.com
http://www.parishprogram.org/matthewhouse.html

Friends of the Children of Lascahobas, Haiti
Estelle Dubuisson
P.O. Box 2047
New York, NY 10025
212-666-4664
info@fclh.org
http://www.fclh.org

Bradley Free Clinic
Estelle Nichols Avner
1240 Third St.
Roanoke, VA 24016
Phone: 540-344-5156
Fax: 540-342-0220
freeclinic@lycos.com
http://www.bradleyfreeclinic.com

Family Service of Roanoke Valley
John Pendarvis
360 Campbell Ave. SW
Roanoke, VA 24016
540-563-5316
info@fsrv.org
http://www.fsrv.org/contact.html

Book Order Form

Book Order Information

Trust Publisher
P.O. Box 872
Salem Virginia 24153

For further copies of The Lambi's Call use this form.
Mail this form with your check to the address above.

Number of Copies to send	#
@ $11.95 each Subtotal	$
$3.05 1st book. $1.05 each additional book. Shipping	$
Total Send check made out to Trust Publisher.	$

For orders over 10 books call for discount. 540-389-3577

Name:______________________________________

Address:____________________________________

____

City:____

State:______________________ZIP:______________

Phone:_____________email:____________________

_____Check if you'd like to schedule an author lecture or presentation for your group. We will contact you.

Book Order Form

Book Order Information

Trust Publisher
P.O. Box 872
Salem Virginia 24153

For further copies of The Lambi's Call use this form.
Mail this form with your check to the address above.

Number of Copies to send	#
@ $11.95 each Subtotal	$
$3.05 1st book. $1.05 each additional book. Shipping	$
Total Send check made out to Trust Publisher.	$

For orders over 10 books call for discount. 540-389-3577

Name:____________________________

Address:____________________________

____

City:____________________________

State:________________ZIP:__________

Phone:__________email:________________

_____Check if you'd like to schedule an author lecture or presentation for your group. We will contact you.